D1595704

READING BONHOEFFER

Cascade Companions

The Christian theological tradition provides an embarrassment of riches: from scripture to modern scholarship, we are blessed with a vast and complex theological inheritance. And yet this feast of traditional riches is too frequently inaccessible to the general reader.

The Cascade Companions series addresses the challenge by publishing books that combine academic rigor with broad appeal and readability. They aim to introduce nonspecialist readers to that vital storehouse of authors, documents, themes, histories, arguments, and movements that comprise this heritage with brief yet compelling volumes.

TITLES IN THIS SERIES:

Reading Augustine by Jason Byassee
Conflict, Community, and Honor by John H. Elliott
An Introduction to the Desert Fathers by Jason Byassee
Reading Paul by Michael J. Gorman
Theology and Culture by D. Stephen Long
Creationism and Evolution by Tatha Wiley
Justpeace Ethics by Jarem Sawatsky

FORTHCOMING TITLES:

iPod, YouTube, Wii Play: Theological Engagements with Entertainment by Brent Laytham
Theological Interpretation of Scripture by Stephen Fowl

Reading Bonhoeffer

A Guide to His Spiritual Classics and Selected Writings on Peace

Geffrey B. Kelly

GEFFREY B. KELLY

To Jean,
With every best personal wish and in gratitude for your loving help to us in the moments of crisis and Susan's illness!
With love and appreciation,
Geff

CASCADE *Books* · Eugene, Oregon

READING BONHOEFFER
A Guide to His Spiritual Classics and Selected Writings on Peace

Cascade Companions 6

Cascade Books
A Division of Wipf and Stock Publishers
199 W. 8th Ave., Suite 3
Eugene, OR 97401

www.wipfandstock.com

ISBN 13: 978-1-55635-236-2

Cataloging-in-Publication data:

Kelly, Geffrey B.

Reading Bonhoeffer : a guide to his spiritual classics and selected writings on peace / Geffrey B. Kelly.

xxx + 168 p. ; 20 cm. — Includes bibliographical references.

Cascade Companions 6

ISBN 13: 978-1-55635-236-2

1. Bonhoeffer, Dietrich, 1906–1945. I. Title. II. Series.

BX4827.B57 K43 2008

Manufactured in the U.S.A.

This book is dedicated in loving memory to Dr. F. Burton Nelson (1924–2004), my soul brother and best friend, who in so many ways exemplified to me and countless others the teachings of Dietrich Bonhoeffer on *Discipleship*, *Life Together*, and the crucial issues of peace and justice featured in this book.

Contents

Foreword

On any short list of theologians who will shape the contours of Christianity in the twenty-first century will be the name of Dietrich Bonhoeffer. While his execution by the Nazis in April of 1945 for complicity in the attempted assassination of Adolf Hitler is perhaps the most dramatic cause for praise and recognition, Bonhoeffer's profound contributions to theology, ecclesiology, and Christian ethics will also prove to be enduring elements of his legacy. For sure, his final sacrifice of life for others served to confirm and authenticate all that he taught and preached.

Similarly, any short list of theologians whose work will influence the direction of Bonhoeffer studies in the twenty-first century will include the name of Geffrey Kelly. We all know that the "generation following after" persons of significance often shapes their legacy in ways inseparable from the legacy itself. Consider Plato's rendering of Socrates, St. Paul's interpretation of Jesus, or Melanchthon's explication of Martin Luther. While Eberhard Bethge (1909–2000), Bonhoeffer's closest friend and later biographer, will remain the most prominent authority offering first-hand history and reliable insights, Geffrey Kelly will certainly stand as one of those in the "generation following after" who brings the breadth and depth needed to insure an authentic picture of Bonhoeffer for the Church of the future. Breadth, because Kelly has offered not only four decades of impeccable scholarship, but also because he has experienced personal relationships with those who knew Dietrich Bonhoeffer first hand; depth, because the theological/spiritual legacy of Bonhoeffer has been Kelly's companion for the same four decades, on the mountain tops and in the valleys. If there is such a phenomenon as God's presence in Jesus Christ being mediated through other persons, Dietrich Bonhoeffer would be one such person, mediating Jesus Christ for, and then through, Geffrey Kelly.

I am deeply honored to be invited to write these introductory words for Kelly's book, and for two reasons. First, he has been for me a mentor in Bonhoeffer studies for thirty years, and I trust these affirmative words will reveal how grateful I am to him for our friendship as well as my affiliation, through him, with the International Bonhoeffer Society. Second, the legacy of Dietrich Bonhoeffer has also been of profound importance for my faith experience and theological orientation. To offer these words of introduction hopefully indicates my gratitude to Dietrich Bonhoeffer as well.

Concerning the text of *Reading Bonhoeffer: A Guide to His Spiritual Classics and Selected Writings on Peace*, I cannot overemphasize its importance for Bonhoeffer studies as well as for the life of the church of Jesus Christ. I hope in this Foreword in some modest way to prepare the readers for an inspirational and educational journey into the life of a truly modern saint, who knew so well that he was also a sinner.

It is no accident that Geffrey Kelly selected *Discipleship* and *Life Together* as the dual foci for this glimpse of Dietrich

Bonhoeffer. While Geffrey could well have used *The Communion of Saints, Act and Being, Ethics, Letters and Papers from Prison*, or *Fiction from Tegel Prison* to introduce Bonhoeffer to the reader, he chose these two pieces because of their organic relationship with each other as well as their primary place in the corpus of Bonhoeffer's writings. Further, by choosing these, he is providing help for a very wide audience, because these two books are surely the most familiar of Bonhoeffer's works. Let me say more about the organic relationship between *Discipleship* and *Life Together*. At the core of Bonhoeffer's preaching and teaching from very early on was his understanding of Jesus Christ as the center of all reality—not least the church—and this reality remained the foundation for his entire theological orientation.

Although nurtured in the bosom of Germany's liberal theological tradition at the turn of the twentieth century, Bonhoeffer's exposure to and experience of the radical-dialectical-crisis theology of Karl Barth was the primary cause leading him to such a Christ-centered vision and vocation. For Bonhoeffer, "following after" (*Nachfolge*) this living Christ into all the world was the essence of discipleship. His theology was not about thoughts or abstractions or principles that were simply to be believed. To know God was to experience Jesus Christ as an active/personal presence in every nook and cranny of life. Intrinsically related to this dynamic understanding of discipleship is the context or setting for such a vocation. *Life Together* (*Gemeinsames Leben*) is the setting and the shape Christian discipleship must necessarily take. Only in community is Jesus Christ experienced and enjoyed! The church, to quote St. Paul, is "the body of Christ." Authentic discipleship always means life together, and authentic life together involves life following after Jesus Christ. I trust that the reader of Geffrey Kelly's book will soon—and significantly—notice this organic relationship between discipleship and life together in a Christian community.

One of Dietrich Bonhoeffer's criticisms of "religion," as it was often experienced and expressed in his day, was that religion compartmentalized life into spheres of sacred and secular, holy and profane, godly and worldly, and with such divisions, created a church out of touch with the world and a world unrelated to God. Against this false bifurcation of reality, Bonhoeffer spoke of God—in Christ—known in the "center of the village," in "strength not only in weakness," and in "life, not only at the time of death." In fact, he understood his involvement in the conspiracy to assassinate Hitler as an act of standing in solidarity with Jesus Christ at the center of life, with all its challenges and curses.

Geffrey Kelly understands deeply and affirms passionately Bonhoeffer's view of "Christ the Center" when he turns our attention in chapter 4 to Bonhoeffer's peace statements and sermons. He knows how closely related Bonhoeffer's convictions about peace were to Christian discipleship and life together. It has been Geffrey's lifelong passion to speak about peace, a passion he shared with his best friend and colleague, Burton Nelson, to whom this book is dedicated. Especially now, at a time in history (2008) when the Bush Administration in America holds up war as a divine crusade, the legacy of Dietrich Bonhoeffer is needed—a legacy that only understands peace to be God's will and war as always a tragic outcome of human failure and sinfulness. Had war been understood as a last resort rather than a tactical choice for retribution, attempting to impose one ideology on another, the current state of world affairs would be quite different. Bonhoeffer's peace writings, shared here by the author, can be of immense help in our day, no less than his.

My hope for you, the readers of this book, who now begin a journey with Geffrey Kelly to and through the life-witness of Dietrich Bonhoeffer, is that the God who became flesh in Jesus Christ will be at the center of your discipleship and life together; that the peace that only God gives, but that virtually every human being seeks in a variety of less-than-fulfilling ways, can finally be experienced as persons follow after Jesus Christ together. I believe both the author and the subject would be disappointed if this book did not somehow draw you, the readers, closer to Jesus Christ and to your neighbor.

John W. Matthews
President of the International Bonhoeffer Society—English Language Section and author of *Anxious Souls Will Ask . . . : The Christ-Centered Spirituality of Dietrich Bonhoeffer*

Preface

My first encounter with Dietrich Bonnhoeffer occurred during the summer of 1964. I was into my second year as spiritual director of postulants, the young men who were aspiring to enter religious life in the congregation of the De La Salle Christian Brothers to which I then belonged. At the time, my own religious life seemed to be in tatters. I was experiencing a dry spell in my prayers and meditations, something like that "dark night of the soul" about which John of the Cross had spoken. My own director advised me to get a different "spiritual reading" book—what we Brothers used back then to "prime our minds" for the daily periods of meditation. Browsing in our novitiate library,[1] I noticed by pure chance the attractive title of a new book on the shelves, *The Cost of Discipleship*—as it was then called—by Dietrich Bonhoeffer. Opening the book at random—not the best way to select

1. Novitiate is the term used to designate the spiritual training of a "novice" in the rules and spirituality of a religious congregation prior to his or her taking the three vows of religious life. In this instance my religious congregation was the "De La Salle Christian Brothers," a teaching congregation originally founded in the seventeenth century in France by Saint John Baptist de La Salle, the patron saint of teachers.

spiritual reading literature!—my eyes fell on the startling sentence: "Like ravens we have gathered around the carcass of cheap grace. From it we have imbibed the poison that has killed the following of Jesus among us."[2] These perplexing words seemed to be addressed directly to me in my uneasy mood that afternoon. I sensed almost immediately that I too had been pursuing the "cheap grace" of a religious routine, a "salvation by works" that Martin Luther had excoriated, as every moment of my day had been carefully mapped out from rising and morning prayers to evening prayers and the "great silence," so much so that Jesus Christ had gradually been fading from the center of my religious life.

I began to read the book from cover to cover and became utterly fascinated by the awesome demands of the Sermon on the Mount that Bonhoeffer had made the centerpiece of the book and with which Bonhoeffer had challenged readers with his electrifying commentary. Through Bonhoeffer's inspirational words Jesus' Sermon on the Mount seemed to be addressed to me personally for the first time. I was hooked. I resolved to learn more about this author and, like so many others, was surprised to find out that the book had been published in 1937 during the repressive dictatorship of Adolf Hitler, and that Bonhoeffer was a Lutheran pastor who had joined the anti-Nazi conspiracy aimed at killing Hitler and overthrowing the Nazi government in order to bring the Sec-

2. This quotation is taken from the new critical edition, *Discipleship* (DBWE 4), 53. In 1964, the text read: "We Lutherans have gathered like eagles round the carcass of cheap grace, and there we have drunk of the poison which has killed the life of following Christ." Bonhoeffer's original text has the word for "ravens" (*die Raben*) not "eagles" and no mention is made of "Lutherans." More on the new translation and critical edition of *Discipleship* later in this book.

ond World War to an end. I was led to the prison letters and then to the story of his execution just three weeks before the end of the war. Even today, many years after that initial encounter, I continue to be deeply moved by the challenges of his writings and by the personal sacrifice of their author.

The opportunity to engage in a more systematic study of the life and writings of Dietrich Bonhoeffer finally came in 1967 when I was assigned to pursue doctoral studies in theology at Louvain University, Belgium. There I was able to work under the noted professor of dogmatic theology, Adolphe Gesché, who had himself for a long time been interested in the issues of a theology of revelation and of Bonhoeffer's radical challenge to the churches as well as to the leaders of those churches and his fellow Christians then caving in to the dictates of Hitler and his fascist ideology. Much research on my part was called for in each of those areas. Professor Gesché's willingness to direct that research made it possible for me to pursue my interest in Bonhoeffer and, through his writings, to study the whole question of the interrelationship of revelation, faith, social ethics, and church.

One pleasant aspect of that research was the opportunity to visit with and come to know the Bonhoeffer family and friends, particularly Eberhard and Renate Bethge. Eberhard was Bonhoeffer's best friend, confidant, the recipient of the prison letters, editor of the posthumous writings, and author of the definitive biography that George Steiner, writing for the *New York Times*, had described as "one of the few assured classics of our age." Renate is Bonhoeffer's niece and daughter of Bonhoeffer's co-conspirator against Hitler, Rüdiger Schleicher, who was himself murdered by the S.S. in the closing days of the war. Renate has been over the years an invaluable source of information about the Bonhoeffer family, her uncle Dietrich, how the family helped to shape Bonhoeffer's attitudes toward the Hitler government, and the role the churches could have played in stopping Hitler and preventing the war's terrible slaughter of the innocent. The Bethges provided me with many of the then unpublished documents that I was able to incorporate into my own work. Eberhard wrote the Introduction to my book, *Liberating Faith*, and the Foreword to *A Testament to Freedom*, which I had co-authored with F. Burton Nelson. Renate wrote the Introduction to *The Cost of Moral Leadership*, also co-authored by F. Burton Nelson, to whom this present book is dedicated. Eberhard died on March 18, 2000, as the manuscript of *Discipleship* was being prepared for publication. Wayne Floyd wrote this testament to his memory in his Foreword to *Discipleship*: "All who meet Dietrich Bonhoeffer in the form of his printed words owe a never-ending debt of gratitude to this remarkable human being. Eberhard Bethge, who almost single-handedly was responsible for assuring that Bonhoeffer's legacy would endure for us and generations to come."[3]

The next great turning point in my development as a "Bonhoeffer scholar" came through my close association with the International Bonhoeffer Society, English Language Section. This development is closely connected with the critical edition of the texts that form the central focus of this book on "Reading Bonhoeffer." Dr. Clifford Green, who had attended an organizational meeting in Germany with Bethge and prominent German scholars in order to found an International Bonhoeffer Society for archive and research

3. Wayne W. Floyd Jr., "Foreword," D (DBWE 4), xiii.

purposes, called a meeting in the Fall of 1972 at his home in Baltimore, Maryland. He had invited John Godsey, author of *The Theology of Dietrich Bonhoeffer*, the first full-length book on Bonhoeffer, Larry Rasmussen, author of the book that analyzed the ethics of Bonhoeffer's role in the anti-Nazi conspiracy, and myself. We were later jokingly referred to as "the gang of four." Be that as it may, we were able to organize the first meeting of an English Language Section of the International Bonhoeffer Society to take place during the 1973 annual convention of the American Academy of Religion, the first of thirty-four sessions that continue to this day. From their inception, these sessions have featured scholars who would present papers on various aspects of Bonhoeffer's theology, ethics, and spirituality, exploring the connection with Bonhoeffer's world and the application of his writings to the problems then besetting our own world. Soon enough we were able to structure ourselves into an official society with standing in the academic world and with regular dues, needed for the annual meeting and for our newsletter. Later we set up a Board of Directors with members elected to the Board and elections held for the positions of President, Vice-President, Secretary and Treasurer. In 1973, before voting procedures were set in place, however, Cliff Green became the first President of the society, and I was named the first secretary and treasurer. Cliff had remarked that it was fitting that the role of treasurer be assigned to me because I was the only member of the growing membership to have taken a vow of poverty! I succeeded Cliff as President for two terms from 1992 to 2000. Michael Lukens, an ecumenical scholar from St. Norbert's College in Wisconsin, was elected to the post in 2000.

For several years the society had been giving equal emphasis to pastoral, spiritual, and ministerial dimensions of Bonhoeffer's theological legacy. It was fitting, therefore, that in 2004, Reverend John W. Matthews, a pastor-scholar from Minnesota and Vice-President of the Society, was elected President to succeed Dr. Lukens. In many ways John Matthews's life and ministry have paralleled Bonhoeffer's own calling as theologian and pastor. In addition to his being senior pastor of Grace Lutheran Church in Apple Valley, Matthews has been active in publishing scholarly articles on Bonhoeffer culminating in his popular book, *Anxious Souls Will Ask . . . : The Christ-Centered Spirituality of Dietrich Bonhoeffer*.

The emphasis in those early years of the society was on counteracting the popular but highly misleading interpretations of Bonhoeffer, such as those suggested by the short-lived "Death of God" movement and efforts to tie Bonhoeffer to political and ecclesiastical agendas not justified by any serious research. To the end of correcting these misinterpretations and presenting Bonhoeffer in texts faithful to his original intent, we directed our energies toward establishing an archive and research center at Union Theological Seminary, where Bonhoeffer's collected writings in addition to significant secondary literature could be housed and made available to scholars, researchers, and anyone else interested in discovering more about the Bonhoeffer legacy. This Bonhoeffer Center was opened in 1977 and continues to sponsor conferences, lectures, and visiting scholar exchanges through cooperation with the German Section of the International Bonhoeffer Society.

Another important function of the English Language Section is, in collaboration with the German Section and all the other national sections, to organize an international congress every four years. These have attracted scholars from around the world interested in exploring further the literary legacy of Bonhoeffer with particular application to the nagging problems that continue to surface—such as militarism, apartheid, fundamentalism, ecumenical dialogue, genocide, etc.—that affect the peoples of the world, so often at the mercy of oppressive, dictatorial regimes. The following congresses have taken place since the first international congress at the World Council of Churches, Geneva, 1976, to commemorate the 70th anniversary of Bonhoeffer's birth: Oxford, England, 1980; Hirschluch, East Germany, 1984; Amsterdam, 1988, New York, 1992; Cape Town, 1996; Berlin, 2000; Rome, 2004. The latest international congress took place in Prague in the summer of 2008. These congresses have produced an international dialogue among Bonhoeffer scholars in addition to publication of critically acclaimed books of the proceedings that have added to further understanding the continuing relevance of Bonhoeffers' writings to national and international issues. They have also led to the cooperation among the various language sections in the production by the International Bonhoeffer Society of new, more accurate translations and critical editions of the entire corpus of Bonhoeffer's literary legacy.

During all those years of scholarly achievement in Bonhoeffer studies our focus as the English Language Section of the society was never far from the desire to produce those new translations and critical editions of Bonhoeffer's collected writings. This project in the English Language Section, the Dietrich Bonhoeffer Works English Edition (DBWE), has been spearheaded by Clifford Green, the society's first president, who was named by the Board of Directors to the position of Executive Director of the series. Green's outstanding leadership has been indispensable in all aspects of the DBWE, including the fundraising needed to assist Fortress Press in financing the extremely large volumes of Bonhoeffer's collected writings that average over seven hundred pages each.

Robin W. Lovin, then of the University of Chicago, was named the first General Editor; he was ably assisted by Dr. Mark Brocker. Before being named Dean of the School of Divinity at Drew University, Dr. Lovin had organized the format of cooperation with the German editors and the process of selecting editors, translators, and consultants for the individual volumes. He was succeeded by Dr. Wayne W. Floyd Jr., who shepherded the first volume, *Life Together*, through to its completion, to be followed by the next six volumes, not in any sequential order. Before volume 8, the long awaited *Letters and Papers from Prison*, could be set in motion, however, Victoria Barnett succeeded Dr. Floyd as General Editor. Barnett is well qualified for the task on two fronts: her fluency in the German language and expertise in the history of the German church struggle that ties into Bonhoeffer's ecclesiology. She has already guided three of the final nine volumes of the project to their completion.

The problem in producing these volumes in English was compounded by the translations already extant of three of Bonhoeffer's most popular, widely read writings: *The Cost of Discipleship*, *Life Together*, and *Ethics*. All of these were deeply flawed by inaccuracies in translations, omissions of entire lines and passages, inconsistencies in translating the original German from one volume to the next, and, perhaps most of all, the absence of the critical apparatus necessary to ascertain the meaning of several otherwise obscure passages. In short, this was a need that pressed on both the German and English language sections. The German section, under the general leadership of Eberhard Bethge and the editorial directorship of Heinz Eduard Tödt and Wolfgang Huber, thus began a systematic production of the individual volumes, assigning each to an expert in that particular book or that collection of essays, correspondence, conferences, sermons, etc., providing for each text an introduction and an "Afterword" as well as the critical apparatus so necessary in understanding the German documents, many only in manuscript notes in need of deciphering. The English Language Section followed suit. Here, though, the process involved not only selecting the scholars for the critical apparatus in consultation with their German language counterparts, but also choosing translators who had to combine expertise in German with a good understanding of Bonhoeffer's theology. As can be seen from the bibliography, this project is still underway, though several of the most significant writings in book form have already appeared, some in a second, paperback edition.

Because of my earlier work in Bonhoeffer's spirituality with particular interest in his writings on Christian community, I was assigned to do the critical English edition of *Life Together*. Prior to this assignment I had to compose a monograph pointing out why a new translation was necessary. Given the unbelievable number of errors in the translation, still being published in its twenty-fourth printing in a widely popular paperback, that part of the task was easy. Also, the inexplicable omission of Bonhoeffer's significant "Preface" or any critical notes only bolstered my argument. This was the first of the volumes to be published in the DBWE. My translator was Daniel Bloesch, with whom I had several friendly exchanges over the translation. Our work, however, had to pass scrutiny from the German editors of the German language edition in consultation with Wayne Floyd, the newly selected General Editor of the entire series. Our collaboration that summer became a model for the further volumes that have combined scholarly insights with accurate notes based on the meaning and context of Bonhoeffer's writings in their German original, illuminated finally by new, fully accurate translations. The commentary on *Life Together* in this book on *Reading Bonhoeffer* is based on my work as editor of that volume in the DBWE.

The second volume to which both John Godsey and I had applied also required a report pointing out the errors in translation of the extant volume, *The Cost of Discipleship*, and the passages in which critical notes were absolutely essential. John and I uncovered at least a hundred errors in translation and were able to make a good case for an expanded critical apparatus based on the German editors' annotations, since each of us had already spent years in researching and teaching Bonhoeffer's book on *Discipleship*. We were also quite familiar with the original German text and the errors in the popular edition. For the next three years we traveled between Philadelphia and Bethesda at work on editing the translation. We were fortunate to have as one of our translators Barbara Green, herself fluent in German and already a published author of articles interpreting Bonhoeffer. She was joined by Reinhard Krauss, a German pastor and scholar, who has had considerable experience working on other volumes in the DBWE. We became a team of four coordinated by the General Editor, as we strived together to produce an accurate, readable and critically annotated volume. This is the volume that serves as the definitive text of *Discipleship* on which that chapter of this book, *Reading Bonhoeffer*, is based.

When I had completed my work on these two volumes, a labor that began in 1993 and ended in 2001, I entertained the idea of writing a separate book to be used as a kind of "Reader's Study Guide" that adult education forums, parish ministries, prayer groups, and spiritual reflection gatherings, as well as regular classes on Bonhoeffer in seminaries and universities, might find useful for their discussions. By 2000, however, I was under contract along with Dr. F. Burton Nelson to write the book, *The Cost of Moral Leadership: The Spirituality of Dietrich Bonhoeffer*. That having been completed and, while I was nearing semi-retired status at La Salle University, I was invited by Jon Stock of Wipf and Stock Publishers to write this book on Bonhoeffer as part of their new series, Cascade Companions. This series was established to make the richness of the vast, complex Christian theological tradition accessible to the general reader. The series addresses this challenge by publishing books on reading and studying in context selected writings of outstanding theologians. Jon sent me the first volume, *Reading Augustine: A Guide to the Confessions*, to give me an idea of what the series was all about. I accepted his offer and, given the nature of the series, decided to narrow my scope down to Bonhoeffer's two spiritual classics, *Discipleship* and *Life Together*.

But because of my own peace activism and my teaching classes and seminars on peace and social justice to both graduates and undergraduates at La Salle University, I decided to include in this "reading-study guide" three of the most thought provoking of Bonhoeffer's collected writings in which he denounced wars and the militarism that was already budding again in his native Germany. Bonhoeffer had used the occasions of a talk presented at an ecumenical conference in Switzerland, a sermon preached on the German Memorial Day, and a dramatic conference presented at a morning service during an important ecumenical gathering in Denmark in 1934, in order publicly to reject war as a denial of Jesus Christ and a rejection of the church's mission to represent Jesus Christ on earth. With uncommon fervor he urged those gathered to hear him to undertake a courageous Christian mission to promote peace in the world at a time when Germany was already engaged in rearming itself under the leadership of Adolf Hitler and when military glory was still being exalted at the expense of fidelity to the teachings of Jesus Christ. These writings are the strongest statements against war that one could ever find in any documents from that troubled period of world history. After composing a biographical first chapter, I have structured the book into three additional sections that deal in turn with *Discipleship*, *Life Together*, and the selected writings by Bonhoeffer on promoting peace against the deceptive allure of war.

Should this book achieve any success among its readership in assisting people to appreciate Bonhoeffer's spiritual classics and his role as a peace activist, it should be noted that I am indebted to several helpful colleagues. First to Clifford Green, Executive Director, for his unfailing leadership and encouragement in the initial phase of the DBWE project and throughout the production of every succeeding volume, now a work of close to twenty years. I have appreciated and benefited from the supervisory assistance of Wayne Floyd, then General Editor, who took the lead in the production of those volumes of the DBWE in which I was involved. My many hours dialoguing with Wayne over how to translate the more difficult passages of *Life Together* helped me in the final crucial months when deadlines had to be met. Wayne's philosophical strengths and his published work on the conceptual foundations of Bonhoeffer's theology in his much earlier Berlin dissertations gave me additional insights into the nature of Christian community life as inspired and directed by Bonhoeffer. My work on *Life Together* did not end there. In writing chapter seven of our book, *The Cost of Moral Leadership*, Burton Nelson and I returned to the volume and had even more intense conversations on Bonhoeffer's text. My commentary on and questions about this text are either based on or drawn from chapter seven of our book. I am indebted to Burton for sharpening my focus, particularly in the application of Bonhoeffer's spirituality of Christian community life to problems in ecclesiology today. Burton died on March 22, 2004, and is sorely missed not only by me but also by his wonderful family and his extended family, his colleagues at North Park Theological Seminary, and in the English Language Section of the International Bonhoeffer Society.

Many of my interpretive commentaries on *Discipleship* are derived from the several exciting discussions on Bonhoeffer's text that I had with my co-editor, John Godsey. We spent countless hours, both formal and informal, refining our understanding of *Discipleship* with its strong Christocentrism and powerful homiletic comments on Jesus' Sermon on the Mount, as well as Bonhoeffer's ecclesial insights drawn from the Pauline letters, among other sources, that became part two of the text. While the commentary is my own, any insights I have been able to share with readers of this book are the fruit of our sessions together. John was himself strongly influenced, as Bonhoeffer had been, by the great Swiss reformed theologian Karl Barth, and has continued his scholarly productivity over the span of nearly half a century. As an Emeritus member of the Board of Directors of the Bonhoeffer Society, John continues to be an inspiration to the young scholars who continue to research Bonhoeffer's theological legacy.

In my classes on Bonhoeffer's Christian spirituality, I am also indebted to my students who were the first to use the discussion questions in their exchanges and debates on how Bonhoeffer's writings applied to their own lives, their churches, and to the United States becoming involved in another war and, to their dismay, in process of being considered a rogue nation by the international community. Some argued that our nation's policies, under our present President, were uncannily similar to what Bonhoeffer had encountered and opposed in the 1930s. As I am entering my senior years and semi-retired status, these students have helped keep my mind fresh and have rewarded me with a sense of appreciation for having introduced them to the inspiring books and other writings that are the grist of this book. I am grateful for their collaboration in the form of questions, reactions, and even the debates with one another on the material of this book as *Reading Bonhoeffer* was taking shape.

I am additionally grateful to Rev. John Matthews, President of the International Bonhoeffer Society, English Language Section, for writing the Foreword to this book. John has been a helpful colleague to me and the entire English Language Section for his scholarly work on Bonhoeffer's Christian spirituality. His election as President of the Society is a tribute to his organizational leadership but more especially for his exemplifying so well the twin aspects of Bonhoeffer's spiritual legacy: scholarly expertise and pastoral care. Like Bonhoeffer himself, John Matthews has been an inspirational light to the churches in their efforts to serve Jesus Christ in what Bonhoeffer called a "world come of age."

The book might never have been completed on time were it not for the skills of my secretary, Yvonne Macolly, who was able to reconstitute chapter 3 that I, still the low-tech anti-nerd, had inadvertently erased from my computer's hard drive and disk.

That the manuscript ever reached publishable form is due in a special way to the expertise of Charlie Collier and Heather Carraher at Wipf and Stock Publishers. Together they did both major and minor surgery on various segments of the text. Their meticulous work was followed by Halden Doerge, who gave the text one final editorial scrutiny for stray sentences in need of further improvement. I am indebted to Charlie, Heather, and Halden for their helpful corrections and perceptive suggestions in producing a more readable text.

Finally, and most of all, I continue to admire the patience of my wife, Joan, and my handicapped daughter, Susan, who kept encouraging me in yet another time consuming project. While Susan never tired of asking me, "Aren't you finished with that book yet?"—an advanced take on her questions during family trips, "Are we there yet?"—still her brand of encouragement added both humor and a sense of urgency to complete the book. But completing the book within the time span allotted by Wipf and Stock needed the time away from home, gardening chores, and assorted other duties that Joan always provided. The book is dedicated to my soul brother,

Burton Nelson, to be sure, but it would have been impossible even to begin without the love and support of Joan, who over the thirty years of our marriage, never ceases to amaze me with her graciousness and forbearance. And to Susan: yes, we are there now!

ONE

Dietrich Bonhoeffer: A Biographical Sketch

Introduction: Bonhoeffer's Place in History

Few people would have ever predicted during his growing-up years in Berlin that Dietrich Bonhoeffer would become part of a political conspiracy aimed at killing the head of state, or a martyr honored around the world for his heroic witness against the murderous ideology of Nazism. In recalling his friendship with Bonhoeffer, Bishop George Bell of Chichester remarked that Bonhoeffer was a moral force for a new Germany. He also reflected on Bonhoeffer's farewell message, delivered through fellow prisoner, the British intelligence officer Captain Payne Best: "I believe in the principle of our universal Christian brotherhood which rises above all national interest."[1] Christian faith, not political expediency, had driven Pastor Bonhoeffer into the German resistance movement and the attempt to assassinate Adolf Hitler and overthrow the Nazi government. Together with other leading members of the conspiracy against Hitler, Bonhoeffer was hanged by the S.S. at the Flossenbürg Death Camp on April 9, 1945, in the waning days of World War II. The cannons of

1. TF, 44; see Best, *Venlo Incident*, 200.

General Patton's army could be heard in the distance. Three weeks later Hitler would commit suicide and the war would be over.

Bonhoeffer was only thirty-nine years old at his death, his influence on the church in Germany seemingly at an end. Yet today, some sixty-three years later, people are still inspired by his *Letters and Papers from Prison*, and especially by his spiritual classics, *Discipleship* and *Life Together*—books that continue to challenge Christians and their churches to follow in the way of Jesus Christ and to resist the national idolatries that masquerade as expressions of Christian faith. In many ways, Bonhoeffer has been even more influential after his martyrdom than he ever was in his brief teaching and preaching career before his participation in the German resistance movement.

Dietrich Bonhoeffer has often been considered a theologian ahead of his time who had pointed his writings to a new phase in Christian thinking that involves a serious questioning of several traditional presuppositions of religion and faith. Many of the original expressions associated with Bonhoeffer, such as "cheap grace" and "costly grace," the "world-come-of-age," "worldly Christianity," "nonreligious Christianity," the "non-religious interpretation of religious concepts," "Jesus the man for others," have become thought-provoking bywords in theology today. Bonhoeffer's prison letters encouraged Christians to reassess the value systems of a nation plunged into the idolatrous nationalism and ruthless militarism that, in effect, denied Jesus Christ and his gospel teachings. Nazi Germany had become engaged in blatant racism, persecution of the so-called "Untermenschen" (those declared to be of less than human worth), and murder of the innocent. Its leaders seemed impervious to human rights while paying homage to their new gods of blood and battle; just war theory had been reduced to an antiquarian idea that they could trim to suit their own aims of world domination. Bonhoeffer's writings remind Christians of their duty to live responsibly, and to courageously oppose, through whole-hearted actions on behalf of the victims, governmentally structured malevolence. Part of the continued fascination with Bonhoeffer stems from the fact that his own life and heroic death are a witness to the sincerity of his teaching. Of few theologians can it be claimed that their lives are fully congruent with their faith and their faith alone, not some secular ideology, acknowledged as the inspiring force behind their religious writings. From prison, Bonhoeffer formulated what to him was the main question that determined the depth of one's faith: "What do we really believe? I mean, believe in such a way that we stake our lives on it?"[2]

Bonhoeffer was born in Breslau, now part of Poland, on February 6, 1906. He was the fourth son and sixth child (his twin sister Sabine was born only moments later) of Paula von Hase, daughter of Karl-Alfred von Hase, preacher at the court of Kaiser Wilhelm II, and Karl Bonhoeffer, a famous doctor of psychiatry, professor at Berlin University, and director of the psychiatric and neurological clinic at the Charity Hospital attached to the university.

Berlin University and Internship in Barcelona

At Berlin University young Bonhoeffer came under the influence of the distinguished church historian, Adolf von

2. LPP, 382.

Harnack, and the Luther scholar, Karl Holl. To the dismay of von Harnack, who regarded him as a potentially great church historian able one day to step onto his own podium, Bonhoeffer instead steered his scholarly energies to dogmatics, where his main interests lay in the allied fields of Christology and Ecclesiology. His doctoral dissertation, *Sanctorum Communio* (The Communion of Saints), completed in 1927, was hailed by Karl Barth as a "theological miracle."[3] Bonhoeffer was only twenty-one years old at the time.

In this dissertation Bonhoeffer describes the church in a memorable phrase: "Christ existing as church community."[4] The uniqueness of Bonhoeffer's thesis lay in his attempt to harness social philosophy to the chariot of ecclesiology, hence his sub-title: "A Theological Study of the Sociology of the Church." Published as a book in 1930, *Sanctorum Communio* reflects a spiritual search that would remain a central concern of Bonhoeffer until the end of his life—namely, to discover the concrete Christian community in which the life of following Christ takes shape. Time and again he would criticize the churches that had seemingly sold their soul to the Nazi ideology. If the church is a "communion of saints," that communion can exist nowhere else but in the congregation of sinners who experience God's graciousness in word, sacrament, and the special gift of being enabled to live for each other. God becomes tangible in the Christian community, where human beings are graced by God and shaped by Jesus Christ into a communion of loving people making visible Christ's incarnate presence as the risen Lord.

3. CML, 8.

4. SC (DBWE 1), 14, 121 et passim.

Not yet at the minimum age for "orders," and in need of practical experience to prepare for his eventual ordination to the ministry, Bonhoeffer interrupted his academic career to accept an appointment in Barcelona, Spain, as assistant curate in a parish tending to the spiritual needs of the German business community. Bonhoeffer's ministry there coincided with the initial shock waves of the great depression. Parish life in Barcelona gave Bonhoeffer his first grim encounter with poverty and stirred him to become a source of hope to those who had lost their means of livelihood. A sermon and a conference from that period urge his parishioners to recognize Christ in the faces of the grubby poor and to ponder the way Christianity teaches the everlasting value of those whom society might castigate as worthless. In Bonhoeffer's words: "Christianity preaches the unending worth of the apparently worthless and the unending worthlessness of what is apparently so valuable. The weak shall be made strong through God and the dying shall live."[5]

Back in Germany, Bonhoeffer turned his attention to the completion of the "second dissertation" required for him to obtain an academic appointment to the university faculty. Published in 1931, *Act and Being* is an in-depth contrast of how revelation, considered as "being," takes place within the Christian community through Christ's continued incarnate presence. But Bonhoeffer also depicts revelation as the "act" of God's eternal word interrupting a person's life in a direct, transcendental way—intervening, often when least expected, to free that person from the narcissistic tendency to turn in on oneself. It seems clear that, throughout the intersecting

5. TF, 52.

analyses of this book, Bonhoeffer wishes to avoid what he saw so blatantly done in church and theology: reducing God to a heavenly double of oneself and God's presence in community to some self-deceiving idolatry whose sole aim was to control God through authoritarian claims of inerrant biblicism or infallible institutionalism. It is clear, too, that Bonhoeffer rejected notions of God's abstract transcendence that place God in heavenly aloofness from creatures. "God is free," he wrote, "not from human beings but for them. Christ is the Word of God's freedom."[6]

HIS YEAR IN THE UNITED STATES AT UNION THEOLOGICAL SEMINARY

Having secured his academic appointment to the university, Bonhoeffer now decided to accept a Sloan Fellowship that offered him the opportunity to travel to the United States for an additional year of studies at Union Theological Seminary in New York City. This year at Union would have an impact beyond the courses he followed. Trying to explain what had happened to him to alter his outlook, Bonhoeffer, in two memorable letters, says simply that he had become a Christian. "I was quite pleased with myself," he wrote. "Then the Bible, and in particular the Sermon on the Mount, freed me from that. Since then everything has changed. . . . It was a great liberation. It became clear to me that the life of a servant of Jesus Christ must belong to the church, and step by step it became plainer to me how far that must go."[7] The effect on

6. AB (DBWE 2), 90–91.

7. TF, 424–25; see also his letter to his older brother, Karl-Friedrich, TF, 423–24.

Bonhoeffer of his close friendships at Union soon became obvious to his family, friends, and students back in Berlin.

Through a black seminarian from Alabama, the Reverend Franklin Fisher, Bonhoeffer experienced firsthand the oppressive racism endured by the black community of Harlem. He also reveled in the caring community and joyful liturgies these people had created for themselves, even in the midst of the great depression's crushing poverty. He spent nearly every Sunday and several evenings with the people of Harlem's Abyssinian Baptist Church. Admiring their life-affirming church services and enchanted by their soulful spirituals, he took recordings of these spirituals back to Germany to play for his students and seminarians. He spoke to them often of the racial injustice that had falsified the boasts of freedom and justice in America.[8] In 1931 he believed that there was nothing analogous to America's racial injustice in Germany. By 1933, however, it was clear to him that Germany's Jews were even worse off than America's blacks.

Gradually, under the influence of another friend, the French pacifist Jean Lasserre, Bonhoeffer came to grips with the tendency of nations to resort to violent solutions, even war, to "solve" their political problems. He came to realize that the dehumanization of the enemy and the hardening of soldiers' hearts to the horror of killing other human beings and of unleashing weapons of destruction against innocent civilians were blatant contradictions of the teachings of Jesus Christ. Lasserre himself recalled that Bonhoeffer began himself to speak passionately about their peace concerns in a way that marked Bonhoeffer as having turned a corner in his at-

8. DB, 155.

titude toward the evils of war and the need for all Christians to embrace Christ's peace on a troubled earth. Bonhoeffer did, indeed, become a consistent opponent of Germany's rearmament and its madcap march toward war throughout the 1930s.[9]

A third friendship, that of Paul Lehmann, had an additional impact on Bonhoeffer's sensitivities then developing through Union Theological Seminary. Paul and his wife Marian became his "American family." Their apartment at Union was perennially available for conversation, sometimes into the late-night hours. Lehmann helped Bonhoeffer deepen his understanding of the need for church involvement in civil rights and the cause of economic justice for those suffering from poverty and degradation in the midst of an affluent America. It was through his profound relationship with Lehmann that Bonheoffer was able to appreciate more fully the insights into social ethics that were being taught by Reinhold Niebuhr.[10] Bonhoeffer's later emphasis on fidelity to Jesus Christ's Sermon on the Mount was undoubtedly influenced by his conversations with Lehmann and his newly found appreciation of Reinhold Niebuhr. Niebuhr's pragmatic approach to the church's role in crafting possible solutions to the problems of social injustice in modern industrial society had a particular appeal to young Bonhoeffer. Later, to paraphrase one of Niebuhr's classic writings, he would be searching for moral people and the restoration of a peace and justice ethic in the midst of an immoral society—Germany under the rule of Adolf Hitler.

9. See Nelson, "Relationship of Jean Lasserre to Dietrich Bonhoeffer's Peace Concerns."

10. TF, 11.

During his return journey from America, Bonhoeffer stopped at Bonn University in order to meet personally with Karl Barth, who had helped to shape his earlier theological education despite the opposition to Barth from von Harnack and his other mentors at Berlin University. Barth had already electrified the theological world through his "Crisis Theology," inspired by a love for the biblical word and permeated with his pungent judgment against the idolatries that, in his opinion, had corrupted the churches and made the "Great War" possible. Barth's courage and impressive mastery of the biblical texts in confronting the churches and their liberal ethics that had caved in to the political ideologies responsible for the war had captivated Bonhoeffer during his student days in Berlin. Now in Bonn, the two became good friends. Later they would be linked in the "church struggle."

Teaching at the University

Once back in Berlin as a young lecturer at the university, Bonhoeffer was able to discuss with his students his ministry to the black youth of the Abyssinian Baptist Church. Wolf-Dieter Zimmermann quoted him saying at the conclusion of one evening gathering: "When I took leave of my black friend, he said to me: 'Make our sufferings known in Germany, tell them what is happening to us and show them what we are like.' I wanted to fulfill this obligation tonight."[11]

Bonhoeffer's teaching career at the university was cast in the shadows of the political and ecclesiastical turmoil that marked Hitler's ascendancy to power. His students admired him for his integrity; some later became his seminarians and

11. DB, 155.

colleagues in the church struggle over accepting or rejecting the Nazi ideology. Those students attracted to Nazism avoided Bonhoeffer. His lectures and seminars began to gather student interest, and beyond that, loyalty. One student wrote that, under Bonhoeffer's guidance, "every sentence went home; here was a concern for what troubled me, and indeed, all of us young people; here was a concern for what we asked and wanted to know." Those who attended Bonhoeffer's classes recalled his spirited analyses of Christian faith and freedom in the overarching context of the call to be daring followers of Jesus Christ. Another student praised Bonhoeffer for what he surmised to be a "Kierkegaardian depth" and an "Harnack-like ability for analysis." This was tempered, the student observed, by a pastoral concern for the students and their needs both spiritual and intellectual.[12]

Bonhoeffer was, in short, noticed as a rising young sensation in the university world. His Christology lectures, presented in the summer semester of 1933 and published in English as *Christ the Center* are, in a way, revealing of how he influenced his students. In those lectures he urged his students to answer the disturbing question: Who is Jesus in the world of 1933? Where is he to be found? Toward the end of the semester, Bonhoeffer reminded his students that Christ had come among them "incognito, as a beggar among beggars, as an outcast among outcasts, as despairing among the despairing, as dying among the dying."[13] The lectures must also be seen in the context of Bonhoeffer's pestering the churches to take the initiative on behalf of the victims of Nazi racist policies.

12. TF, 80.

13. TF, 122; CC, 107.

Ordained on November 15, 1931, Bonhoeffer found time from his academic load at the university to teach catechism to a group of young confirmands in the slum section of Prenzlauer-Berg. He left a lasting impression on these lads who were crowded into one of the poor sections of Berlin and had already been exposed to the drumbeats of the Hitler Youth Movement. To be more involved in their problems, he moved into their neighborhood, visited their families, and invited the boys to spend weekends at a rented cottage in the more peaceful mountainous area of Biesenthal.

The Church Struggle

During this period Bonhoeffer was more and more appalled at the attempt of Hitler, aided by some enthusiastic Nazis among church leaders themselves, to integrate racism, militarism, and blind patriotism into official church policy, and to refuse to defend publicly both the human dignity and civil rights of those ordinary citizens targeted for persecution by the Nazis. This led to the schism that split the Protestant churches of Germany into several opposing factions. Those who adopted Hitler's national socialism as part of their creed became known as "German Christians" and their church, the "German Reich Church." This church seemed to view Hitler's National Socialism as "positive Christianity in action."[14] The infamous "Brown Synod" of 1933—so called because so many of the clergy showed up wearing brown shirts and sporting the swastika—elected as national Bishop the Nazi sympathizer, Ludwig Müller. The delegates, not surprisingly,

14. LF, 22.

adopted the "Aryan Clause" denying the pulpit to ordained ministers of Jewish blood.[15]

Even before the church elections, at the beginning of April 1933, Bonhoeffer took steps to pressure the church to resist the government decrees that had excluded Jews from civil service and sponsored the boycott of Jewish stores. Bonhoeffer's talk to the clergy of Berlin, entitled "The Church and the Jewish Question," urged the churches to risk entering into open conflict with the state by, first, boldly challenging the government to justify such obviously immoral laws. Secondly, he demanded that the church come to the aid of the victims and not fret about whether they were baptized or not. Finally, he declared that the church should "jam the spokes of the wheel" of the state should the persecution of this people continue.[16] Such an outspoken defense of the Jews was a rarity in Nazi Germany. His remarks angered several of the clergy present at his talk. But Bonhoeffer and his group of "Young Reformers" had taken the more drastic step of asking their churches to call a General Council to condemn the heresy of the German Reich Church and even to declare spiritual interdict, shutting down the sacramental systems until the racially motivated laws within both church and state were abolished.[17]

A stronger church opposition to Nazi racism was organized shortly after the Brown Synod in the form of the "Pastors Emergency League." Bonhoeffer and the decorated hero of the "Great War," Pastor Martin Niemöller, met in Berlin at the home of the young pastor, Gerhard Jacobi, to declare a

15. TF, 17–18.

16. TF, 132.

17. TF, 16.

state of emergency within the church. Together they pledged to fight for a repeal of the Aryan Clause and for a "Confession of Faith" that would not only attack the rising idolatrous acquiescence to Hitler but also expose the heretical nature of the Reich Church. By late September 1933, at the National Synod of Wittenberg, they had obtained two thousand signatures in support of their movement. But, to Bonhoeffer's disappointment, the Bishops again remained silent. Only later, at the Barmen Synod of May 29–31, 1934, which marked the official beginning of the Confessing Church, was there a robust enough opposition to the Reich Church. One important clause of the Barmen Confession of Faith, drawn up in large part by Karl Barth, clearly identified the Nazi ideology as tantamount to idolatry: "We repudiate the false teaching that there are areas of our life in which we belong not to Jesus Christ but to other lords, areas in which we do not need justification and sanctification through him."[18]

Even before Barmen, Bonhoeffer and a fellow "Young Reformer," Pastor Hermann Sasse, had been commissioned to withdraw to the retreat center of Bethel and to compose a "Confession of Faith" that could openly challenge the German Christians. The document, known as the "Bethel Confession" was in its original form a solid, uncompromising declaration of the theological basis of the church struggle and a stirring defense of the Jewish people now being pilloried by a spurious, official racism in both church and state. Unfortunately, before being circulated, the "Bethel Confession" was so watered down to make it less offensive to a majority of pastors

18. TF, 20.

and the government that in the end Bonhoeffer himself refused to sign the final toothless version.

London and Ecumenical Activities

At this juncture, Bonhoeffer took leave from his teaching post at Berlin, a university that, to him, seemed more and more to have yielded to the popular mood that hailed Hitler as a political and economic savior. He was also disturbed by the university's failure to defend the Jewish professors whose positions were threatened by anti-Jewish legislation. These included his brother-in-law of Jewish ancestry, Gerhard Leibholz, a young teacher of Law, married to his twin-sister, Sabine. Despite his baptismal certificate, Leibholz had been dismissed from his teaching position at Göttingen University. Bonhoeffer departed for England to assume the pastorate of two German-speaking parishes in the Sydenham section of London, where today the Dietrich Bonhoeffer Church is located.

From the more distant vantage point of London, Bonhoeffer used his ecumenical activities not only to publicize the Barmen Confession of Faith but also to rally the churches to take a stronger anti-Nazi stand. Bonhoeffer had been appointed International Youth Secretary of the "World Alliance for Promoting International Friendship through the Churches," a forerunner of the World Council of Churches. His work on this new front led to his lasting friendship with Bishop George Bell of Chicester, President of the "Universal Christian Council for Life and Work." With Bishop Bell's help, Bonhoeffer was able to alert the churches to the dangers to which the faith of the Protestant Church was exposed. In his letter to Bishop Bell of March 14, 1934, Bonhoeffer urged the Bishop to help their Pastors Emergency League through some form of solidarity in their cause. "The question at stake in the German church," he wrote, "is no longer an internal issue but is the question of existence of Christianity in Europe; therefore, a definite attitude of the ecumenic[al] movement has nothing to do with the 'intervention' [should Bell be accused of intervening in an internal affair of Gemany]—but it is just a demonstration to the whole world that church and Christianity as such are at stake."[19]

Bonhoeffer's repudiation of the German Reich Church reached a climax at the ecumenical conference held in 1934 in Fanø, Denmark. Bonhoeffer and other members of the Ecumenical Youth Commission astounded the typically staid delegates by their refusal to couch resolutions in easily ignored, polite diplomatic language. They dared the delegates to behave with uncharacteristic courage on the issue of how churches were being manipulated and co-opted by political ideologies. All the delegates knew that the German Reich Church was the target of Bonhoeffer's critique.

In that phase of the ecumenical movement that deals with the Fanø conference, Bonhoeffer was most vividly remembered for his memorable morning conference on peace, entitled "The Church and the Peoples of the World." In that session he rejected attempts to soften Christ's gospel of peace. The church, he declared, had to be in the vanguard of a movement to establish peace in the world. He added that "this church of Christ exists at one and the same time in all peoples, yet beyond all boundaries, whether national, politi-

19. TF, 399; to read Bonhoeffer's correspondence with Bishop Bell in this period, see TF, 394–403.

cal, social, or racial." The churches had a mandate from none other than Jesus Christ to prohibit wars. One sentence of that sermon remained forever emblazoned in the memories of Bonhoeffer's students: "Peace must be dared; it is the great venture!"[20]

The Seminary Director

For a long time Bonhoeffer had been pondering whether his efforts to outlaw war might be better served by adopting as his own the tactics Gandhi had used so successfully against the British empire. He began, therefore, to make plans to visit India in order to learn firsthand about Gandhi's way of life and his nonviolent resistance to evil. Thanks to strong recommendations from both Bishop Bell and Reinhold Niebuhr, he was accepted as a disciple in Gandhi's Ashram. However, the trip to India would remain a dream never to be realized. Instead, having been approached by leaders of the Confessing Church on the possibility of his becoming director of an illegal seminary to be located in Pomerania, Bonhoeffer chose an entirely different kind of resistance to the Hitlerian ideology—that of training seminarians to be a subversive element in Nazi Germany.

The young seminarians, who gathered first at Zingst on the Baltic Sea and later at an abandoned private school in Finkenwalde, near Stettin, remembered Bonhoeffer's seminary as an oasis of freedom and peace. They soon discovered two things about Bonhoefer and his understanding of the gospel: his desire that they form themselves into a genuine

20. TF, 228–29.

Christian community and his anti-militarism bordering on pacifism.

In his insistence on community, Bonhoeffer structured the typical seminary day around a regimen of common prayer, meditation, biblical readings and reflection, fraternal service, and his own lectures. The highlight of their training remained, however, Bonhoeffer's reflections on the Sermon on the Mount, which his biographer, Eberhard Bethge, has called the "nerve center" of the seminary.[21] Bonhoeffer had to defend his manner of training the seminarians against those who were quick to see in the "common life" at that seminary certain "catholicizing" tendencies. In answer to his critics, Bonhoeffer pointed out that in the short time of their seminary training, "the brethren have to learn . . . how to lead a communal life in daily and strict obedience to the will of Christ Jesus, in the exercise of the humblest and highest service one Christian brother can perform for another; they must learn to recognize the strength and liberation to be found in brotherly service and communal life in a Christian community."[22] The Gestapo closed down the seminary in October 1937. Bonhoeffer was alerted by his brother, Karl-Friedrich, not to return to the seminary lest he be arrested by the Gestapo.

The spirit of Finkenwalde has survived, however, in two books that reached the outside world, *Discipleship* and *Life Together*. *Discipleship* was the outgrowth of Bonhoeffer's lectures to his seminarians on the Sermon on the Mount and on the Pauline exhortations to take one's faith seriously enough to accept even death for the sake of Jesus Christ. In this text,

21. DB, 450.

22. TF, 26.

too, we read of Bonhoffer's denunciation of "cheap grace," a phrase that Christians to this day have found challenging to any moral complacency on their part. *Life Together*, published in 1939, was a recording for posterity of the "experiment in community" that was the concrete form Bonhoeffer and his seminarians had given to a reform of the typical church life in Germany then under the heel of Adolf Hitler. The church, Bonhoeffer insisted, needed to create more genuine Christian communities such as he and the seminarians had experienced in order for new life to be breathed into their belligerent, paganized society.

FRUSTRATIONS IN THE CHURCH STRUGGLE

During the years 1937 to 1939 Bonhoeffer's essays and lectures were brimming with bitterness over the failure of nerve on the part of church leaders. He was outraged that these same leaders were not only accommodating to their criminal government but also shirking their responsibility to protest the unjust treatment of dissenting pastors and the even harsher measures against Jews in direct violation of their basic human rights. He would frequently quote Proverbs 31:8, "Who will speak up for those who have no voice?" to explain why he had to be the "voice" defending the Jews in Nazi Germany.[23]

By autumn 1938, however, Bonhoeffer felt that he was a man unsupported by his church. He was frustrated in his efforts to influence church leaders to take a stand against the Nazi government that he had come to regard as inherently evil. But other problems were looming on his horizons as Germany seemed bent on preparation for war.

23. Bethge, "Dietrich Bonhoeffer and the Jews," 69–70.

The events of Kristallnacht (Crystal Night), November 9, 1938, in which the full fury of Nazi anti-semitism was unleashed on the Jewish citizenry, further convinced him of the apathy and ineptitude of the churches when it came to issues of social justice. Bonhoeffer was away from Berlin on that night, but he quickly raced to the scene of the wanton destruction of property and terrorizing of Jewish citizens. He angrily pointed out the maliciousness of attributing this violence to God's so-called curse of the Jews because of the spurious claims of their "killing of Christ." Bonhoeffer's seminarians remember his vehement prediction that, "if the synagogues are set afire today, tomorrow the churches will burn," as he insisted that Crystal Night was of a piece with Nazi contempt for Christianity as well as Judaism. In his Bible he underlined the words of Psalm 74:8: "they say to themselves: let us plunder them! They burn all the houses of God in the land" and marked it with the date of Crystal Night.[24]

A Second Journey to America

Bonhoeffer's disaffection with the spineless leadership he had come to detest in the churches was one of the factors that led him to contemplate a second trip to America. A more pressing reason for leaving Germany was the imminent call to the army of his age group. His friends, who knew of his pacifist leanings and his rejection of Nazi ideology, could only expect that he would refuse military service, though this could mean imprisonment and execution and tend to bring down more Nazi wrath on his colleagues in the Confessing Church. Hence his closest American friend, Paul Lehmann, and his

24. Bethge, "Dietrich Bonhoeffer and the Jews," 74–75; TF, 32.

former teacher, Reinhold Niebuhr, formed a committee of two to arrange for a lecture tour. Their intention was to insure a safe haven in America for Bonhoeffer once the impending war had begun. Bonhoeffer accepted their invitation and embarked for the United States on June 2, 1939.

However, having gained the coveted distance from the ecclesiastical and civil turmoil that was clouding his life, Bonhoeffer now longed to be more involved in the anti-Nazi action back home. He soon made up his mind to thank his American hosts and return to Germany as soon as possible. He departed on July 8, 1939, a mere month after his arrival. The reasons for his change of mind are expressed in a farewell letter to Reinhold Niebuhr and his American friends. Bonhoeffer's words are an inspiring statement of his heroic decision to accept the dangerous mission in his own country to which God was calling him. "I have made a mistake in coming to America," he wrote. "I must live through this difficult period of our national history with the Christian people of Germany. I will have no right to participate in the reconstruction of Christian life in Germany after the war if I do not share the trials of this time with my people."[25]

Joining the Conspiracy against Adolf Hitler

On his return home he found himself isolated from the public forum he had as a pastor and teacher. Under suspicion for his association with the Confessing Church, he was forbidden to teach, to preach, or to publish without submitting copy for prior approval. He was also ordered to report regularly to the police. The freedom to continue his writing came un-

25. TF, 479–80.

expectedly through his being recruited for the conspiracy by his brother-in-law, Hans von Dohnanyi, and the central figure in the anti-Hitler conspiracy at that time, Colonel Hans Oster, who arranged to have him listed as indispensable for their espionage activities. This move gained him the needed exemption from the military draft and removed him from Gestapo surveillance in Berlin. Bonhoeffer had become officially an unpaid double agent for the "Abwehr," German Military Intelligence.

Though his ostensible mission was to scout intelligence information for the military through his "pastoral visits" and ecumenical contacts, Bonhoeffer used that cover as a secret courier and agent for the resistance movement. These included "Operation 7," a daring plan by the Abwehr to smuggle some prominent Jews out of Germany and to inform the outside world of Nazi atrocities. It was this rescue attempt in the Abwehr's complex web of anti-Nazi actions that initially attracted the Gestapo's suspicions and eventually led to Bonhoeffer's arrest.

Bonhoeffer's principal mission, however, was to seek terms of surrender from the Allies should the plot against Hitler succeed. The highpoint of these negotiations between the resistance movement and the allies came at the secret rendezvous with Bishop Bell in Sigtuna, Sweden, in May 1942. Through Bonhoeffer, Bell was convinced that the conspirators could be trusted to carry through the plot to assassinate Adolf Hitler, overthrow the Nazi government, restore democracy in Germany and make war reparations. He conveyed that information to Anthony Eden, Great Britain's Foreign Minister. Unfortunately, both Churchill and Eden had hardened themselves into what had become the Allied battle cry of those years: "Unconditional Surrender!" Bell would later complain that a more statesmanlike response to Bonhoeffer's proposal could have helped the conspirators, hastened the end of the war, and saved millions of lives.[26]

WORK ON *ETHICS*, ARREST, AND IMPRISONMENT

Bonhoeffer also used the cover of his "espionage duties" in another way. Headquartered in the Benedictine Monastery of Ettal, Bavaria, he was able to continue writing what he once declared to be his main life's work, his *Ethics*. In this book, Bonhoeffer addresses the great moral dilemmas posed by the war and the need to arouse the Christians of Germany to a greater sense of responsibility in shaping their own historical destiny. Bonhoeffer challenges his readers to set before themselves the example of Jesus Christ and to ponder the ethical ramifications of searching for the ways in which Christians can conform to Jesus Christ in their war-torn, genocidal world. On the question of the Nazi persecution of Jews, he reminds his nation that, "driving out the Jew(s) (*Juden verstossung*) from the West must result in driving out Christ with them, for Jesus Christ was a Jew."[27]

For many readers the most unsettling section of Bonhoeffer's *Ethics* lies in his upbraiding the church through a "Confession of Guilt" for their involvement in the Nazi atrocities. In the church's name Bonhoeffer confesses that it "has witnessed the suffering of countless innocent people, that it has witnessed oppression, hatred, and murder without raising its voice for the victims and without finding ways of

26. CML, 29.

27. E (DBWE 6), 105.

rushing to help them." And, in a stinging phrase that demanded the churches own up to their complicity in the Holocaust, he declared the church "guilty of the lives of the weakest and most defenseless brothers and sisters of Jesus Christ."[28] This was Bonhoeffer's euphemism for the persecuted Jews and the imprisoned pastors. What is especially astounding in this "Confession" is that it was composed while Germans were dancing in the streets and hailing their "fearless leader," Adolf Hitler, and joyfully celebrating the greatest of all German victories, the fall of France. In the midst of all the cheering Bonhoeffer was privately lamenting the church's role in the suffering on which Nazism's military glory fed.

Bonhoeffer was arrested by the Gestapo on April 5, 1943, and incarcerated at Tegel military prison in Berlin. Though at first the Nazis had only vague charges against him, such as his evading the military draft, his role in "Operation 7" and his prior "disloyalties," the full truth of his part in the plot against Hitler emerged after the failure of the July 20, 1944, assassination attempt. It was in his correspondence from Tegel prison that Bonhoeffer raised the disturbing questions that confronted the disturbing irrelevancy of the churches when it came to speaking a prophetic word against the violence and that shattered the smug assumptions of so many theologians in the post-war period. In these *Letters and Papers from Prison* Bonhoeffer is harsh on those churches that had diluted the gospel and softened the demands of faith in order to insure their survival as church and to preserve their privileges. For Bonhoeffer, the churches' failure to respond to the cry of

28. E (DBWE 6), 139.

a people trapped in the killing fields of a world at war was to deny Christ anew.

Letters from Prison

The tone of Bonhoeffer's theological reflections in these letters is set in the letter of April 30, 1944, in which he confides that, "what is bothering me incessantly is the question of what Christianity really is, or indeed who Christ really is, for us today."[29] In responding to that question, Bonhoeffer observed that the church, anxious to preserve its clerical privileges and survive the war years with its status intact, had offered people only a self-serving religious haven from personal responsibility. The churches of Nazi Germany were hardly the visible representation of the presence of Jesus Christ unafraid to disturb the peace of political overlords. Nor did the churches exhibit any moral credibility for a "world come of age" that no longer needed the tutelage of religion to solve problems once considered to be solely in the domain of the deity and the ecclesiastical establishment. In these letters Bonhoeffer saw the world entering a time of "nonreligious Christianity." This, he said, called for a nonreligious interpretation of biblical concepts in which Christ's lordship of the world could be honestly addressed in terms shorn of their pietistical otherworldliness. The church had to shed forever those "religious trappings" so often mistaken for authentic faith and face up to the tough questions of what it really believed in, and for what cause it was willing to sacrifice its life.[30]

29. LPP, 279.

30. See TF, 491–522.

The inspiration that animates Bonhoeffer's urging the churches to come out of their stagnation and risk entering into controversy is that of Jesus Christ, whom he portrays as "the one for others." For Bonhoeffer, if Jesus is the "man for others," then the church can be the church only when it exists to be of service to people.[31] The cutting edge of God's judgment on the church, according to Bonhoeffer, is set in the gospel's radical affirmation of the meaning of the cross of Jesus Christ. The church had to follow Christ to that cross if it were ever to reclaim its credibility and once again proclaim God's word against the idolatries that had led to the murder of the innocent in the battlefields and the death camps. A church bearing the name of Christ could not be permitted to play it safe in a time that called for courageous compassion and sacrifice. Bonhoeffer scornfully chided church leaders for failing to speak the prophetic word or to do the responsible deed for fear of losing what the following of Christ most demanded of them, the sacrifice of their respected status and privileges and, if need be, their lives.

Through these letters Bonhoeffer became more famous after his death than he could ever have hoped to be during his brief teaching and preaching career in the years prior to his joining the anti-Hitler conspiracy. After their publication Bonhoeffer seemed to belong to the world at large. In them we can observe a young pastor and teacher deeply in love with his people and brave enough to risk his life in a struggle with both church and country for peace, justice, and fidelity to the gospel.

31. See LF, 125–27.

Last Days and Execution

What we know of the last days of Bonhoeffer are gleaned from the book, *The Venlo Incident*, written by a fellow prisoner, the British Intelligence officer, Captain Payne Best. Bonhoeffer and Best were among the "important prisoners" who on April 3, 1945, were loaded into a prison van and transported southward to the "death camp" at Flossenbürg. On April 8th they reached the tiny Bavarian village of Schönberg where the prisoners were herded into the small schoolhouse then being used as a temporary lockup. It was Low Sunday and several of the prisoners prevailed on Bonhoeffer to lead them in a prayer service. He did so, first offering a meditation on Isaiah's words, "With his wounds we are healed." Then he read the opening verses of the First Epistle of Peter: "Blessed be the God and Father of our Lord Jesus Christ! By his great mercy we have been born anew to a living hope through the resurrection of Jesus Christ from the dead." In his book Best recalled that moment: "he reached the hearts of all, finding just the right words to express the spirit of our imprisonment, and the thoughts and resolutions which it had brought."[32]

Their quiet was immediately interrupted as the door was pushed open and two Gestapo agents entered and demanded that Bonhoeffer follow them. For the prisoners this had come to mean only one thing: he was about to be executed. Bonhoeffer took the time to bid everyone farewell. Drawing Best aside, he spoke his final recorded words, a message to his English friend, Bishop Bell of Chicester: "This is the end—for me, the beginning of life. Tell him . . . with him I believe in the principle of our universal Christian brotherhood which

32. TF, 44; Best, op. cit., 200.

rises above all national interests, and that our victory is certain—tell him, too, that I have never forgotten his words at our last meeting."[33]

Early the next morning Bonhoeffer, Wilhelm Canaris, Hans Oster, Karl Sack and three others of their fellow conspirators, were hanged at the "death camp" of Flossenbürg. The camp doctor who had to witness the executions remarked that he watched Bonhoeffer kneel and pray before being led to the gallows. "I was most deeply moved by the way this lovable man prayed, so devout and so certain that God heard his prayer."[34]

The Nazism Bonhoeffer fought against would linger on, however, in a Nazism of the heart, in postwar militarism, blind patriotism, corporate greed, and other forms of systemic evil that continue to torment peoples in the modern world. Bonhoeffer's legacy to the churches is a challenge to view the world through the person of Jesus Christ who made common cause with the hated Jew, the dispossessed poor, and the vilified outcasts of a mean-spirited society. This is poignantly expressed in a Christmas message in which he reminded his fellow conspirators that they were acting in solidarity with all the victims of Nazi malevolence. "We have for once learned to see the great events of world history from below, from the perspective of the outcast, the suspects, the maltreated, the powerless, the oppressed, the reviled—in short, from the perspective of those who suffer."[35] Such a Christlike identity with those who have been crushed by powerful political and economic ideologies and militaristic malevolence is the cen-

33. TF, 44.

34. TF, 44.

35. LPP, 17.

terpiece of Bonhoeffer's life and the most inspiring message of his theological and spiritual legacy.

QUESTIONS

1. Dietrich Bonhoeffer is famous for his resistance to Nazism in general, and the regime of Adolf Hitler in particular. What lesser-known aspects of his story interested you?
2. Do you see a connection between Bonhoeffer's prophetic resistance to Nazism in Germany and his deep love for the black church-community in Harlem? Explain.
3. When you imagine Christian ministers in training, do you think of a place like Finkenwalde? If not, is Finkenwalde more or less attractive to you than your image of seminary life? Why?
4. Christians in Western democracies continue to be arrested and imprisoned by their governments for activities subversive to the state. Do you know who some of these people are? Do Bonhoeffer's life and witness make you curious about fellow citizens who have like Bonhoeffer given up their liberty for the sake of the gospel?

TWO

On Reading Bonhoeffer's Spiritual Classic, *Discipleship*

History of the Text

Originally published in German in 1937 as *Nachfolge* ("Following after" [Christ]), *Discipleship* was the first of Dietrich Bonhoeffer's books to be published in English translation. Endowed with the catchy title, *The Cost of Discipleship*, the book appeared in 1948 in abridged form as a collaborative effort initiated by Bonhoeffer's brother-in-law (married to Bonhoeffer's twin sister, Sabine), Gerhard Leibholz, who also wrote an introductory "Memoir" that placed the book in its biographical and historical context. Bishop George Bell of Chicester, Bonhoeffer's closest friend from Great Britain and confidant during the church struggle, contributed the Foreword. The American edition, enriched by Reinhold Niebuhr's preface, was published by Macmillan Company a year later. This edition was also abridged. To the dismay of scholars the abridged versions had omitted ten sections of Bonhoeffer's original German text.

Those sections were restored in subsequent publications beginning with the SCM edition of 1959 and that of the

Macmillan Company in 1960 as well as the paperback editions in 1963 (Macmillan) and 1964 (SCM). In 1995, Simon and Schuster purchased the rights for its Torchback paperback edition. Although Irmgard Booth had revised Reginald Fuller's original translation for the editions of 1959 and 1960, from their inception, all editions of *The Cost of Discipleship* have been marred by faulty, misleading translations and the absence of the critical notes needed to understand why *Discipleship* is so pivotal in appreciating Bonhoeffer's intent more fully.

To that end, the International Bonhoeffer Society, English Language Section, inaugurated the Dietrich Bonhoeffer Works Translation Project (DBWE) of which *Discipleship* is the fourth volume in what will eventually be seventeen volumes of Bonhoeffer's collected writings. Each volume provides readers with an entirely new, unabridged translation coupled with the critical apparatus lacking in previous translations but now supplied by experts skilled in interpreting Bonhoeffer and familiar with the individual texts assigned to them. The present text of *Discipleship*, edited by John D. Godsey and Geffrey B. Kelly and published in 2001 by Fortress Press, is based on the critical German edition published in 1989 and revised in 1994. That critical edition was in turn based on the first edition of 1937, though improved through corrections of typos and other printing mistakes. The new critical edition illumines Bonhoeffer's role in writing the book as an important document in the church struggle in the Hitler era. In addition, the critical apparatus explains many of the historical allusions otherwise left to the imagination of the reader and subject to misinterpretations. Finally, *Discipleship* relates Bonhoeffer's text to the inner core of his Christocentric spirituality.

The Opening of *Discipleship*: Cheap Grace and Costly Grace

At the outset of *Discipleship*, Bonhoeffer makes it clear that he wants to get behind the ideological battles related to the church struggle and focus on the one person who ought to be the center of their concerns, Jesus Christ. He poses the disturbing question: "What does Jesus want from us today?" As a caution against what the churchgoing Germans were hearing from their pulpits, academic podiums, or reading in their newspapers, Bonhoeffer concludes in this opening section: "It is not ultimately important to us what this or that church leader wants. Rather, we want to know what Jesus wants."[1] *Discipleship* is a book in which Bonhoeffer uses Jesus' own words as recorded in the gospels and the exhortations of the apostle Paul to confront readers with the uncushioned challenges to all their inaccurate ideas, falsified by Nazi propaganda, of what it means to be a follower of Jesus Christ. Although the book was first published in 1937, the words that have excited each new generation of readers were actually spoken or written much earlier, during Bonhoeffer's work as a young teacher in Berlin and as a seminary director in lectures to his seminarians. In writing *Discipleship* Bonhoeffer drew on the insights he had expressed in prior writings and lectures on church, faith, and community life in order to integrate a Christ-centered spirituality into the demands on their daily lives of those who proclaim themselves followers of Jesus Christ.

The book itself was set in its penultimate form during his years as director of the illegal Confessing Church seminary at

1. D (DBWE 4), 37.

Finkenwalde in Pomerania. There Bonhoeffer was able to present his thoughts more fully on following Jesus Christ in the paths of Christian discipleship. Bonhoeffer's biographer and best friend, Eberhard Bethge, called Bonhoeffer's reflections on the Sermon on the Mount the "nerve center" of the seminary and the book that ensued, "Finkenwalde's own badge of distinction."[2] In those lectures he opened to his seminarians the personal heart of his own spirituality: discipleship and the cross, living out the teachings of Jesus Christ even if that led to their persecution and martyrdom. The opening passages of his book expose his deeply felt chagrin at the church's apparent watering down of Jesus' teachings and example in their efforts to accommodate a powerful political ideology. He shares his conviction that too many church leaders had cheapened the gospel and misled their parishioners. The protestant principles of faith alone, scripture alone, and giving glory to God alone now had deteriorated into mere boorish churchgoing, easy procurement of sacramentalized grace, and reduction of the Bible and worship to abstract dogmatics, legalisms and routine rituals.

Cheap Grace, the Mortal Enemy of the Church, and Costly Grace in Discipleship

The first chapter of the book that created such a stir both in Germany and, later, in the English speaking world, begins with Bonhoeffer's declaration of the real source of the crisis generated by the collapse of any effective church resistance to Adolf Hitler and the growing popularity of Nazism among the citizens of Germany: "Cheap grace is the mortal en-

2. DB, 450.

emy of our church. Our struggle today is for costly grace."[3] Bonhoeffer goes on to describe this "cheap grace" as "bargain basement" Christianity doled out by careless and cowardly church leaders, in the form of doctrines, principles, systems, a cheap "cover-up for its sins" for which the church "shows no remorse." It is, in effect, the denial of the word of God and everything Jesus Christ stands for. Finally, the cheapening of grace reaches the point of denying the need to follow Jesus Christ in discipleship. It is devoid of the cross and "without the living, incarnate Jesus Christ."[4] Jonathan Sorum has said it well: "Cheap grace is *not* grace and Costly grace is *simply* grace."[5]

In this initial chapter Bonhoeffer then turns his attention to a contrast between cheap grace and costly grace. Costly grace is simply the gospel that can never be taken for granted but is subject to daily renewal. He says it is costly because it is the call to follow Jesus Christ, a path that can cost Jesus' followers their lives. Such grace condemns sin, though through Jesus it offers justification to all sinners who repent. Such grace was even costly to God because it cost the life of God's own son whose death was a sacrifice for us. Later, Bonhoeffer will write in his prison letters of this aspect of God's own sufferings. Here he concludes that "costly grace is the incarnation of God."[6] As God's living word, costly grace places people of faith under the yoke of actually following Jesus, a yoke that Jesus himself declares to be "easy" and "light."[7]

3. D (DBWE 4), 43.
4. D (DBWE 4), 43–44.
5. Sorum, "Cheap Grace, Costly Grace, and Just Plain Grace," 20.
6. D (DBWE 4), 45.
7. Matt 11:30, cited in D (DBWE 4), 45.

Bonhoeffer traces costly grace to Jesus' threefold call to Peter to follow him. Peter was asked to follow Jesus, to confess his faith in Jesus, and finally, to enter into the communion of martyrdom. But such examples were gradually lost through the twin developments of Christendom's expansion and the advent of secularization. Monasticism came into existence as a protest against this cheapening of grace and toleration of human sin. Those involved in the monastic movement left everything for the purpose of following Jesus' commands more strictly. But monasticism itself lost its impact, suffocated at the hands of the very church it had protected from the decay of creeping secularization. The church began to exalt this way of following Christ to the province of only those few individuals, a specially graced elite who were so called, whereas the average churchgoers were steered toward the easy, watered down way of believing in Jesus Christ. Enter Martin Luther who, by leaving the monastery was himself led to protest against the corruption of discipleship. Returning to the world, he was enabled by God's grace to declare that following Jesus had to be extended to all peoples living their lives in the midst of the world. His new allegiance to Jesus Christ had cost him a comfortable monastic life in favor of finally understanding the true nature of justification by faith alone that in turn became living the gospel in the world in discipleship to Jesus Christ alone. The church itself would begin to sink into its own addiction to a status quo of wealth and privilege.

Nonetheless, as Bonhoeffer goes on to point out, the forces searching for an easier way to be Christian reduced the dynamism of justification by faith alone into a principle whereby sinning was justified in advance and following Jesus became no different from being like the world, thoroughly secularized. Christianity was further cheapened by churchgoing seen as a social gathering where one leaves the worldly sphere for a short time to enter a church service and receive assurance that one is on the right track of discipleship. This, for Bonhoeffer, is the gross deception that parades as justification but in effect constitutes a falsified liberation from the gospel demands of Jesus Christ. Luther's paradoxical call to "sin boldly" when construed as a presupposition of justification had, to Bonhoeffer's dismay, become a preset absolution merely to do as one pleases and to bask in a discounted form of discipleship.

Bonhoeffer could see the results in Nazi Germany when so many parishioners were afraid to "sin" against the status quo of political structures that denied human and civil rights to their fellow citizens or against the churches that had acquiesced in the violence of the Nazi government. Hence his caustic denunciation of the disturbing effects of pursuing a cheapened Christianity: "Like ravens we have gathered around the carcass of cheap grace. From it we have imbibed the poison which has killed the following of Jesus among us."[8] He concludes with a litany of lamentations on the consequences of pursuing cheap grace. Bonhoeffer had become convinced that the churches' influence for good had collapsed. Bland preaching and an easy self-righteousness based on mere church attendance had so cheapened Christian life that the call to follow Jesus Christ by accepting the gospel challenges had become diminished. The leaders of Nazi Germany were thus able successfully to erect barriers against actions on be-

8. D (DBWE 4), 53.

half of justice for peoples trapped in a repressive, militaristic ideology.

The Call to Discipleship and Simple Obedience

Bonhoeffer's analysis in his second chapter of the dynamics of Jesus' call to follow him delves into the gospel stories of those who have, indeed, either risked all to accept the call or succumbed to the temptations of evading the stark demands of the call or even invoked reasons to reject the call. Bonhoeffer insists that the essence of the call is that it comes from none other than Jesus himself and it compels obedience without the usual rationalizations that might impede the directness of the call itself. The promptness of Levi's obedience from Mark 2:14 illustrates what Bonhoeffer means by the content of the call to discipleship. The disciple leaves everything. Disciples step out of their previous existence and livelihood and embrace the insecurity of where Jesus might lead them while paradoxically enjoying the absolute security that communion with Jesus confers. Jesus' call breaks through all the legalisms, dogmatic systems, and rationalizations because the call is to a person. In Bonhoeffer's words: "Discipleship is commitment to Christ."[9]

Answering the Call without Hesitation

Bonhoeffer contrasts Levi's answer to the call with the examples one finds in Luke's gospel story of three would-be followers of Jesus. The first simply declares he will follow Jesus. Jesus gives him in return a reality check. Following him will

9. D (DBWE 4), 59.

not be easy. He has no set place to lay his head. Nor would the would-be follower qualify who would first bury his father according to the law. The issue in that case is to prefer obedience to the law to the call of Jesus. Here Bonhoeffer comments that nothing, not even the law, should come between Jesus and the disciple. One suspects that Bonhoeffer is alluding to the conflict so prevalent in the Nazi era that following Jesus Christ could very well entail violating laws that the gospel would oppose. Finally, a third would-be follower wants time to bid farewell to his family. This provokes Jesus' reply about the unworthiness of one who would put his hand to the plow and looking back, probably with regret, on what he had left behind. Bonhoeffer interprets this to mean Jesus' refusal of a discipleship in which the would-be follower sets his own conditions for accepting the call. This, he declares, is tantamount to a rejection of what Jesus wants in favor of one's own will.[10]

Bonhoeffer then addresses the question of what comes first, the gift of faith or the graced obedience to the call of Jesus Christ. Here he steps into the controversy that reaches all the way back to the Reformation, justification by faith and not by works. Like Luther, Bonhoeffer argues that good works are not eliminated in the response to Jesus' call. In fact, they emanate from the faith that justifies. Bonhoeffer makes the daring statement in this chapter that "the road to faith passes through obedience to Christ's call." For Bonhoeffer, the Christian life is not a choice between the priority of faith and obediential discipleship. Faith and obedience are correlative: "*only the believers obey* and *only the obedient believe*."[11]

10. D (DBWE 4), 60–61.

11. D (DBWE 4), 63; emphasis Bonhoeffer's.

He admits that the obedience in question follows on faith and that the actions done in obedience do not in themselves justify either sinners or would-be disciples. Nonetheless, he sees an "indissoluble unity between faith and obedience."[12] Obedience to Jesus' call or command is of crucial importance in this dialectic. Otherwise, he argues that faith could easily deteriorate into pietistic and deceptive abstraction and the external actions in accord with Jesus' mandates on behalf of the "least" of society's children could more easily be downplayed and avoided. That would be the "cheap grace" behind which so-called believers in Christ could hide, safe in being absolved from obeying Jesus' difficult gospel demands.[13]

The Problem of the Rich Young Man

Bonhoeffer uses the story of the rich young man who wanted, like so many contemporary believers, to parse Jesus' call to completely change his priorities in favor of an unconditional willingness to follow in Jesus' own way that could include, as it did for the rich young man, voluntary poverty. Jesus, as the gospel reports, loved him but recognized at the same time that the young man wanted something more concrete in the way of ethical laws or behavior, never realizing that the call was to leave his affluence and follow the person of Jesus wherever that could lead, even to an unknown future. The scribe's question, on the other hand, was all about the relative standing of God's commands for salvation. Again, his probing into gauging the worth of the salvific commands of God betrays an inability to imitate Jesus in extending neighborly love to all

12. D (DBWE 4), 64.
13. D (DBWE 4), 69.

those who in Jesus' spirit may lay claim to one's compassion and help.[14]

Bonhoeffer's third chapter extends his analysis of the call to discipleship to the issue of "simple obedience." Jesus' call has to circumvent several seemingly inbred obstacles: the dictates of reason, common sense, the invocation of personal responsibility, one's personal, comfortable piety, legal hesitations, and even scripturally cited reasons to evade the call. Bonhoeffer's answer is simplicity in obedience to the call. When Jesus calls a person to follow him, one is not to be deterred like the rich young man by worldly possessions or personal wealth. Jesus' call, on the other hand, can mean leaving one's present station in life, one's family and home, and friends, all of which are outweighed by the fulfillment of entering into community with none other than Jesus Christ.[15] The disciples who answer the call are told not to worry. Every source of anxiety, such as worry for the family or even how to respond to being struck in the face by an enemy, should give way to the primal nature of Jesus' call, namely, the promotion of God's Kingdom on earth as it is embodied in Jesus' personal example and teachings.[16]

Bonhoeffer concedes that one could argue the possibility of living in the world while possessing the world's goods as if one did not possess them and still believe in Christ. But he argues further that such a possibility can never annul or satisfy simple obedience to the gospel commandments. There is always the danger, he points out, in one's worldly attachments, affections, or affluence that they can become

14. D (DBWE 4), 72–76.

15. D (DBWE 4), 78–79

16. D (DBWE 4), 79.

a pretext for fleeing from obedience to Jesus Christ when his demands appear to escalate beyond one's comfort zone. Bonhoeffer continues to insist that what seems impossible in human terms becomes, in faith, a willingness to engage in gospel-inspired actions. The word of God can thus thrust persons of faith into such actions and provide them the helping grace they need in the face of danger and despite their all-too-human fears.

Simple Obedience in Uncompromising Discipleship

Bonhoeffer's emphasis on "simple obedience" was not new to him. In an earlier talk that he gave to young students involved in the German Student Christian Movement in Berlin in 1932, entitled "Christ and Peace," he had declared that refusing to follow the path of obedience to the gospel teachings is only to "make grace cheap and with the justification of the sinner through the cross of Christ, we thereby forget the cry of the Lord who never justifies sin." He added the following uncompromising comment that is echoed in his later book on *Discipleship*: "The command, 'you shall not kill,' and the word, 'love your enemy,' are given to us simply to obey. . . . Simple obedience knows nothing of the fine distinction between good and evil. It lives in the discipleship of Christ and does the good work as something self-evident."[17]

According to Bonhoeffer, in such situations legalisms are of little help. Nor can ideals offer the guidance that can only come from Jesus' call and Jesus' graced commands. Other forms of obedience, whether to law or to ideals, might trap people within themselves and enslave people of weak faith within political or religious ideologies and patriotic slogan-

17. TF, 94–95.

eering as was evident in the historical era in which Bonhoeffer was writing. He concludes that salvation through discipleship to Jesus Christ is ultimately possible only through God's costly grace and not through any merely human endeavor.[18]

Discipleship and the Cross of Jesus Christ

In chapter 4 Bonhoeffer subsequently connects Christian discipleship to the cross of Jesus Christ. This is the sobering reality of how far the call of Jesus Christ can take a would-be follower. This chapter is pivotal to discipleship, given the widespread persecution by the Nazi government of Jewish citizens, political dissenters, and anyone suspected of disloyalty to the regnant political ideology, including Bonhoeffer's own Confessing Church. Many of Bonhoeffer's fellow pastors had been imprisoned and the moves against the Jews were already in place aimed at expelling or annihilating the entire Jewish population in Germany. Though the genocidal implementation of Hitler's "final solution" to the "Jewish Question" was only a few years away, Hitler's evil intentions were already clear to Bonhoeffer and those who would become his fellow conspirators in the German resistance movement.

Bonhoeffer contends from the very beginning of this chapter that Jesus *had* to "suffer and be rejected." The suffering was tragic enough, but the rejection was even more painful. "Rejection removed all dignity and honor from his suffering. It had to be dishonorable suffering. Suffering and rejection express in summary form the cross of Jesus."[19] Bonhoeffer admits that not all Jesus' followers were at peace with Jesus'

18. D (DBWE 4), 81–83.
19. D (DBWE 4), 85.

declaration that he was destined to suffer. He notes that even Peter rejected this role immediately after his remarkable confession of faith in Jesus' messiahship. For this friendly persuasion, Jesus rebuked Peter in some of the harshest words one finds in the scriptures (Mark 8:33). Bonhoeffer sees Peter as exemplifying the church's own offense at the suffering of Christ. Here, we see how Bonhoeffer uses Jesus' rebuke to Peter as a lament at the cowardice of the churches, afraid of suffering in the manner of Jesus for taking a courageous stand against Hitler and the Nazi government. He calls that the work of Satan "trying to pull the church away from the cross of its Lord."[20] In his letters from prison, Bonhoeffer will complain that the church was "standing up for the church's 'cause', but [with] little personal faith in Christ. 'Jesus' is disappearing from sight. . . . The decisive factor: the church on the defensive. No taking risks for others."[21]

According to Bonhoeffer, Jesus makes it clear to his followers that they too must be prepared to suffer. True, the disciples are free in their choices, but *if* they intend to follow Jesus, they will suffer. In preparation for such a gospel-predicted eventuality Jesus counsels his followers to practice self-denial. This Bonhoeffer describes as the grace of "knowing only Christ, no longer knowing oneself,"[22] in the sense of keeping oneself always secondary in following Jesus who tells them unmistakably that all his disciples must take up their cross. Keeping Jesus foremost in one's thoughts makes the pain of the cross endurable because the cross of Jesus Christ is itself grace just as the preparation through acts of self-denial

20. D (DBWE 4), 85.

21 LPP, 381.

22. D (DBWE 4), 86.

is also a grace that Jesus confers on those who answer the call with sincerity and courage.[23]

The Cross of Rejection

Bonhoeffer depicts Christ's death on the cross as a sign for disciples of their calling, as followers of Jesus Christ, to accept sufferings as essential to their vocation. In communion with the passion of Jesus, the cross of Christians also brings on them rejection, shame, and desertion by one's own people. We can only wonder if Bonhoeffer had in mind the shame and rejection experienced by those Christians accused of a lack of patriotism, of disloyalty to Adolf Hitler, of making common cause with the hated Jew. Or, would his words come back in his own case, when he faced accusations of treason for planning the overthrow of his evil government and death by hanging as a traitor? Or was he thinking of the churches and their bishops so craven in their attempts to win favor with the Nazi government and to retain their clerical privileges?

In Bonhoeffer's commentary he assures readers that there is no need to seek out a particular cross to bear. God's benevolence will know each person's weaknesses and thus measure the personal cross accordingly. Some may be honored with the grace of a bloody martyrdom. But for Christians the cross is laid on all, whether it is the death of one's old self and ways of conduct or the renunciation of every earthly attachment in order to follow Jesus wherever he leads. The cross that Jesus experienced in rejection and death is the destiny of every true disciple of Jesus Christ. In Bonhoeffer's stark words: "Whenever Jesus calls us, his call leads us to death."[24]

23. D (DBWE 4), 86–87.

24. D (DBWE 4), 87.

Like Jesus, Christians are asked to take up as their cross even the sins and guilt of others in bearing the burdens from which Jesus' present day brothers and sisters still suffer. Bonhoeffer likens this bearing of burdens to the forgiveness of sins, so necessary if reconciliation in the midst of society's sins and the presence of one's enemies as a path toward peace can ever be realized. Paul's injunction would thus be obeyed that Christians bear one another's burdens in order to fulfill the law of Christ (Gal 6:2).[25] Bonhoeffer cites Luther who counted suffering as one of the "marks of the true church." He refers also to the Augsburg Confession, which "defined the church as the community of those 'who are persecuted and martyred on account of the gospel.'" He adds a stringent warning that "those who do not want to take up their cross, who do not want to give their lives in suffering and being rejected by people, lose their community with Christ."[26]

DISCIPLESHIP AND THE INDIVIDUAL

In a Germany in which Adolf Hitler and the Nazi leaders capitalized on mass hysteria, fear mongering to induce conformity, and the lure of blind patriotism to achieve Germanic unity for their policies, Bonhoeffer's emphasis on the individual disciple in chapter 5 offered a sobering counterbalance. Here Bonhoeffer declares that the individual followers of Christ must decide for themselves in solitude and alone. In fact, he insists that Christ calls each person alone, and in the process makes that person into a genuine individual. This, he argues, is the point of Luke 14:26; the disciple must make

25. D (DBWE 4), 88.
26. D (DBWE 4), 89.

the difficult decision to leave behind father, mother, and the entire family including one's associates.[27]

According to Bonhoeffer, none other than Jesus Christ makes that break possible. The familial and national fractures created by choosing Christ are not traceable to some prescribed law of nature, society, or some form of contempt for such ties; rather these fractures are, in reality, the graced movement toward and commitment to Jesus Christ alone above the ties of blood and nation. The gospel thus becomes the medium through which God, not the immediacy of the world and its gods, encounters the human person and makes effective a new way in which the world is seen and confronted by those who follow Jesus Christ. Bonhoeffer frowns on what he calls "immediate relationships," in which the sinful barriers between the world that crucified Christ and the disciple are broken down to the advantage of those who would blind believers to the dark side of all worldly attachments and sap the stamina of those who declare faith in Jesus Christ alone.[28]

In this connection Bonhoeffer cites the example of Abraham, called to sacrifice his son Isaac. Trusting in God's word, Abraham's obedience to God through the sacrifice of his son involves a drastic repudiation of the natural ties that impede unconditional obedience to God. Abraham returns, gifted with Isaac's life but completely changed in his attitude toward the world and its values. In this he models discipleship in Christ since followers of Christ must likewise leave everything behind to enter with a purified vision into the Christian community.[29] Refreshed with the grace of Jesus Christ, they

27. D (DBWE 4), 92.

28. D (DBWE 4), 95–96.

29. D (DBWE 4), 97–98.

encounter their family and nation anew. These faithful disciples then stand through the strength of their newness of life and with a purified individuality in a faith community whose spirit is that of Jesus Christ. They see the world and their ministry with the vision that is the life and death of Jesus Christ and his gospel word. Bonhoeffer concludes with a powerful statement on how such discipleship is ultimately rewarded. "Those who left their fathers for Jesus' sake will surely find new fathers in the community, they will find brothers and sisters; there are even fields and houses prepared for them. Everyone enters discipleship alone, but no one remains alone in discipleship. Those who dare to become single individuals trusting in the word are given the gift of church-community. They find themselves again in a visible community of faith, which replaces a hundredfold what they lost."[30] He adds the obvious that this gift includes persecution.

THE SERMON ON THE MOUNT AND THE BEATITUDES

For Bonhoeffer, being bonded to the sufferings of Jesus Christ extended not only to persecution and the ultimate sacrifice of one's life but also to the daily acts of renunciation that define the beatitudinal grace of Christian discipleship. Bonhoeffer declares that the beatitudes are the point of convergence where discipleship and the cross, the sufferings of Jesus and the power of Christian community, faith and love of neighbor, come together. Jesus proclaims that his followers are blessed in what the world would call misery: poverty, meekness, sorrowing, rejection, sufferings, persecution, even death at the hands of one's enemies. This is the paradox of joy in suffering,

30. D (DBWE 4), 99.

life in death, that only the graced intimacy with Jesus Christ, not any political or social program, could bring about. It is the paradox of the "fullness of grace" that confers the interior joy of sharing in God's sufferings while caught in the midst of what the world calls destitution and distress.

Bonhoeffer's commentary on the beatitudes is unique in the context of Nazi Germany's malicious grip on the citizens of Germany and their churches. Indirectly, he provides guidelines for a genuine Christian life even when surrounded by the world whose values proclaim a state of enmity to Jesus Christ and his gospel teachings. Beginning with Jesus' declaration that the poor are blessed, Bonhoeffer sees in this beatitude the voluntary renunciation of wealth that could provide a more comfortable existence. Instead, the followers of Christ choose freely to live in want, insecurity, and in separation from worldly enticements in order to live solely for Jesus and the Kingdom of God on earth. Their "treasure" is a hidden affair discovered in their embracing the cross. Here he contrasts Jesus' blessing of the poor with the political-social programs initiated by the Nazis. Bonhoeffer heaps scorn on the hypocrisy of the Nazi party's efforts for the poor of Germany that many churches had praised. For Bonhoeffer the work of the "Antichrist" could be seen in the ways the Nazi party with all its wicked designs on expanding its ideological influence among the masses, was parading under the masquerade of doing good.[31] As far as his seminarians were concerned, this beatitude was especially important since they had agreed to serve in the anti-Nazi Confessing Church, dependent on free-

31. D (DBWE 4), 102–3.

will donations, with all the stigma of disloyalty constantly cast at them.

Those who mourn are blessed, for example, because they are not caught up in the world's definitions of happiness and peace. They mourn the idolatries of their secularized world. They are unwilling to conform themselves to society's standards or to join in arrogant celebrations while the country parades its own economic prowess, military might, and futuristic achievements as the real kingdom of God on earth. Christians, he points out, are to be strangers in that phony world and, in the name of the only true peace of Jesus Christ, disturbers of that false peace and blind patriotism based on belligerent arrogance toward weaker nations that the enemies of Christ seek to dominate by military conquest.[32]

Bonhoeffer likewise wrote that the death of Jesus Christ paralleled the death to self-righteousness endured by those who would be merciful. In Bonhoeffer's spiritual outlook, following Jesus to death entailed a renunciation even of one's own personal dignity. Those who embrace the beatitudinal way of compassion, he declared, "share in other people's need, debasement, and guilt." Christians join the ranks of the disenfranchised by making common cause with those reprobated and marginalized by their government. He praised those who, despite their own needs, "have an irresistible love for the lowly, the sick, the suffering, for those who are demeaned and abused, for those who suffer injustice and are rejected, for everyone in pain and anxiety. They seek out all those who have fallen into sin and guilt. No need is too great, no sin is too dreadful, for mercy to reach. The merciful give their honor to

32. D (DBWE 4), 103–4.

those who have fallen into shame and take that shame unto themselves."[33] On reading those lines one can in the contemporary world reflect on the contemporary example of Sister Prejean, whose ministry to those on death row in prisons of the United States where the death penalty is still enforced, despite the teachings of Jesus Christ, himself a victim of capital punishment. One wonders, too, if Bonhoeffer's convictions here might have influenced his decision to join the conspiracy and make common cause with those who had to accept the "guilt" of being considered traitors to their country and its head of state, Adolf Hitler.

Concerning the beatitudinal blessing on those who become advocates for peace in the face of war, Bonhoeffer states in the starkest of terms what Jesus is demanding of his followers. "Jesus followers are called to peace. When Jesus called them, they found their peace. Jesus is their peace." But this "peace" was not the self-righteous contentment that, because they proclaimed Jesus as savior, automatically bathed them in the abundant grace of a salvation untouched by the troubles and evils of their society. Bonhoeffer makes it clear that the grace of following Jesus Christ as peacemakers has a strong responsibility to oppose violence by nonviolent means as Jesus would. "Now they are not only to have peace, but they are to make peace. To do this they *renounce violence and strife*. Those things never help the cause of Christ." How far are Christians to take this beatitude? For Bonhoeffer, in a direction that many Christians would find unthinkable. "Jesus' disciples maintain peace by choosing to suffer instead of causing others to suffer. They preserve community when others destroy it. . . .

33. D (DBWE 4), 106–7.

Their peace will never be greater than when they encounter evil people in peace and are willing to suffer from them. Peacemakers will bear the cross with their Lord, for peace was made at the cross."[34] These words on the call to act as truly "children of God" in the cause of world peace find their echo in the nonviolent efforts on behalf of human dignity, freedom from oppression, and recognition of civil rights by Martin Luther King, Mohandas Gandhi, and Archbishop Romero, in their own graced efforts to follow Jesus Christ on behalf of their persecuted people.[35] In an earlier sermon, Bonhoeffer called peace "the great venture" that "must be dared."[36] His words were a challenge to the ecumenical delegates crafting ways to iron out their differences in order to achieve forms of church unity and cooperation. What better cause for Bonhoeffer than disarmament and proclaiming the peace of Jesus Christ against a world hell-bent on war and imperial domination?

As for the persecution that followers of Jesus Christ can and should expect, Bonhoeffer says that this refers to the necessity in the Christian ministry to take up the cause of justice and righteousness. In so doing, followers of Christ will inevitably give offense to the world. They can expect suffering and rejection and, in this, be blessed like the poor in the first beatitude. He asks where on earth does one find the kind of faith community that will agitate on behalf of the poor, compassion, peace, and justice except at the foot of the cross. In Bonhoeffer's words: "The faith community of the

34. D (DBWE 4), 108.

35. See Kelly, "Who Stands Firm?" 5–6.

36. TF, 228–29.

blessed is the community of the crucified. With him they lost everything, and with him they found everything." He goes on to explain the why and how of the persecution followers of Christ will endure if they live the beatitudes. "Things cannot go any other way than that the world unleashes its fury in word, violence, and defamation at those meek strangers. The voice of these poor and meek is too threatening, too loud. . . . In their poverty and suffering, this group of Jesus' followers gives too strong a witness to the injustice of the world. That is fatal."[37]

The Visible Church-Community and Jesus' Righteousness

In the ensuing sections Bonhoeffer comments on the remaining verses of Matthew's redaction of Jesus' Sermon on the Mount. Once again, the background of his analysis lies in Hitler's having co-opted the churches to his own vision of Germanic glory. If the church is called to be the salt of the earth and the light of the world, its sad decline in influence over parishioners in Nazi Germany stands in contrast with Jesus' beatitudinal mandates to his followers. Bonhoeffer saw the churches fleeing into a virtual invisibility at a time when courage, not craven timidity, was called for. Hitler would rather that the church hide its light under Nazi bushel baskets, lest the darkness of his own vision be exposed and the conformity of the masses to the Nazi ideology be opposed by a force as powerful as the churches.[38] Bonhoeffer adds a flurry of rhetorical questions that argue for a visible church

37. D (DBWE 4), 109–10.

38. D (DBWE 4), 110–14.

witness to Jesus Christ creating a light that can be shined on Nazi duplicity and injustice. "Is the cross conformation to the world? To the shock of everyone else, is the cross not something which became outrageously visible in the complete darkness? Is it not visible enough that Christ is rejected and must suffer, that his life ends outside the city gates on the hill of shame?"[39] It bothered Bonhoeffer that the churches of Germany chose political quietism over their prophetic vocation to confront evil and denounce infidelity to Jesus Christ's gospel teachings.

There then follows Bonhoeffer's exposé of how Jesus' own righteousness can be lived on the practical level and the law fulfilled in the newness of life with which Christ graces his followers. This "better righteousness" forbids the anger that can escalate into violence even within one's own family. Achieving reconciliation is Jesus' mandate for defusing anger and avoiding violence of all sorts.[40] Bonhoeffer's commentary here stands in unmistakable contrast with Hitler and his fellow Nazis's encouraging vengeance and fomenting fear of one's enemies both within and without Germany as prelude to their plans to destroy those "enemies."

Bonhoeffer goes on to discuss the need for self-denial and self-control, particularly in matters of how a man relates to a woman. The way is open to liberate marriage from lust and to strengthen the bonds of marriage through faith. But Bonhoeffer also sees the way open for one to renounce marriage—at that time Bonhoeffer himself was considering renunciation of marriage in light of his all-embracing ministry

39. D (DBWE 4), 114.

40. See D (DBWE 4), 119–24.

in Nazi Germany—to be even more single-minded in commitment to Jesus Christ.[41]

Next, Bonhoeffer applies Jesus' mandate always to be truthful and to refuse to takes oaths. While conceding the function of oaths in civil affairs, nonetheless Bonhoeffer expresses his concern here for the loyalty oaths so prevalent in Nazi Germany whether in government office, the military, civil service, and even the church vis-à-vis the government. The Reich church, in keeping with its professed loyalty to the Nazi ideology, had demanded such an oath for pastors and church officials. Bonhoeffer rejected this decree and refused to obey it. His words reveal his staunch opposition to the ways the churches went out of their way to accommodate the Nazi government, unwittingly conferring undeserved respectability on Hitler and National Socialism. "Thus, for the sake of truthfulness and following Jesus, it is impossible to swear such an oath without the reservation of submitting it to the will of God. For Christians, there is no such thing as absolute earthly allegiance. A loyalty oath which intends to bind a Christian absolutely is a lie that comes 'from the evil one.'"[42] When, in 1938, a similar oath of allegiance was demanded by Dr. Friedrich Werner, state commissar for the Prussian Church, as a sign of their patriotic loyalty and as a birthday gift from the church to Adolf Hitler, the synodal leaders of the Confessing Church went into crisis mode and by majority vote decided to leave the taking of such an oath to the individual pastors. Bonhoeffer railed at the church leaders because their decision would have exposed the dissenting pastors to dismissal and reprisals from the Gestapo. His letter

41. See D (DBWE 4), 125–27.

42. D (DBWE 4), 130.

to the church leaders was brimming with anger in the series of questions he addressed to them. "Will Confessing Synods ever learn that it is important to counsel in the peace and patience commanded and to decide in defiance of all dangers and difficulties? Will they ever learn that majority decision in matters of conscience kills the spirit?"[43]

RETRIBUTION AND ATTITUDES TOWARD THE "ENEMY"

Following the lead of Jesus Christ, Bonhoeffer coupled his plea that Christians and their churches undertake the cause of peace with the need to forgive and pray for their enemies. Bonhoeffer was struggling to establish a critical Christian presence in the world. He was a vigorous critic of the church's apparent yielding to the seduction of the Nazi millennium. His commentary on the "abundant grace," however costly, in obeying Jesus' call in the Sermon on the Mount, included what in Nazi Germany was considered highly suspicious and unpatriotic—pacifism. Bonhoeffer insisted that Christians are not to repay in kind the evil done to them. Instead, evil was to be overcome by suffering without retaliation. His conviction that injustice is overcome by nonviolence and even forgiveness led Bonhoeffer to several radical statements that are in turn a challenge to Christians today. Americans live in a culture that is dominated by vengeful, violent attitudes toward personal enemies, incarcerated criminals, and unfriendly, ideologically opposed nations. Yet Bonhoeffer insists in his commentary on Jesus' sermon that Christians' attitudes toward enemies reflect the extraordinary love that Jesus himself manifested and enjoined on his followers. That is why Jesus

43. TF, 465.

commands his followers to "pray for those who abuse and persecute" them. Such forbearance and love is what Jesus had asked of his followers in declaring that their righteousness had to be different from and more than the so-called goodness of the Pharisees and Sadducees, with their legalistic, minimalist approach to religious faith. With Jesus' extraordinary forbearance in mind, Bonhoeffer insisted that what is distinctly Christian be manifested in the extraordinary love, self-denial, and espousal of nonviolence and forgiveness of enemies. Hence Jesus' counsel to his followers to pray for and forgive one's enemies and to do good to those who hated and persecuted them (Matt 5:43–48).

This spirit of forbearance was reinforced by St. Paul who in Romans 12 would add his own advice to bless those who curse Christians and not to refuse food or drink to one's enemies. According to Bonhoeffer, these very attributes set Christians apart from those urged on by their political leaders to hate enemies, to be self-indulgent materialists, to deny the truth and dignity of the peoples they abuse, and to be led into wars of aggression. He pinpoints the uniqueness of Christianity as the cross of Jesus Christ, which allows Jesus' followers to transcend all the vile standards of a powerful but heartless society.[44] Bonhoeffer goes so far as to add some strange and unique rhetorical questions by way of motivation in following Jesus Christ down this path of forgiving one's enemies. These may be especially apropos today, given the background of so many societies like Nazi Germany and even the United States in recent times that appear to relish taking revenge on their enemies. For Bonhoeffer, unforgiving revenge

44. See D (DBWE 4), 137–45.

is a violation of the teachings about loving and forgiving enemies that one finds in the gospels. Bonhoeffer appears to radicalize this directive even more. "But who needs love more than they who live in hate without any love? Who, therefore, is more worthy of my love than my foe? Where is love praised more splendidly than amidst love's enemies?"[45] Earlier in his career Bonhoeffer was particularly incensed at the trumped up cause of "national security" as a pretext for nations to engage in an arms race as prelude for another war. In an earlier address at an ecumenical gathering of delegates to the World Alliance for Promoting International Friendship through the Churches, meeting in Gland, Switzerland, five months before the Hitler takeover of power in Germany, Bonhoeffer called national security an "idolatry."[46]

ON THE HIDDEN NATURE OF THE CHRISTIAN LIFE

Having already strongly argued for a visible presence of Jesus' followers as a light for the world, Bonhoeffer now turns to the dangers of misinterpreting that call to visibility and proceeding to create a species of church triumphalism and holding up for admiration a public exaltation of the extraordinariness of certain pietistic lifestyles. Such tactics, he complained, could make Jesus out to be an "enthusiast" or a "revolutionary extremist" seeking "to turn the world upside down" by leaving the world to 'build a new world."[47] Bonhoeffer detects a spiritual arrogance that demeans the everyday ordinary behavior of Christians who follow Christ in genuine humility.

45. D (DBWE 4), 139.

46. TF, 104.

47. D (DBWE 4), 147.

Rereading Jesus' own words, Bonhoeffer concludes that Jesus was diffident about external deeds of which a would-be follower might boast. The "better righteousness" of Jesus, on the other hand, looked to the heartfelt intentionality of Jesus' followers. This was necessarily foreign to the self-sanctification that could destroy the church-community with its hubris and prideful self-exaltation. Bonhoeffer quotes Jesus' own warning: "Beware of practicing your righteousness before others in order to be seen by them" (Matt 6:1). Following Christ in this perspective demands critical reflection on whether the extraordinary, even courageous deeds may deviate into a sinful desire just to be seen and rewarded with human praise. Bonhoeffer acknowledged the paradox of doing the necessary deeds to enlighten a world mired in the mud of an evil ideology, yet with the intention of looking solely at Jesus Christ and affirming that they act out of simple obedience to the Lord. The cross of Christ illustrates what can at the same time be visible and yet hidden. According to Bonhoeffer, the disciple of Christ must exercise "exclusive allegiance to Jesus Christ. . . . The only required reflection for disciples is to be completely oblivious, completely unreflective in obedience, in discipleship, in love."[48]

Bonhoeffer preached and taught at a time when everywhere the extraordinary visibility of the church should have elicited a prophetic stand against the violence and injustice proclaimed as lawful and necessary by Adolf Hitler and the Nazi government. To oppose this bold, seductive attempt to corrupt the German citizenry to follow their leader down an immoral pathway required a simplicity of obedience to the

48. D (DBWE 4), 150.

gospel of Jesus Christ. Given the dangers of defying the Nazi government, there would predictably ensue the incarceration and even death of the follower of Jesus Christ and even the public destruction of the churches. But, in Bonhoeffer's view, that simple obedience derives from "death to the old self" which, though "no longer alive," permits Christ to live anew in the person of faith.[49] One might ask with Bonhoeffer why the churches that so readily preach resurrection should fear death on the crosses erected by nations like Nazi Germany to frighten them away from active dissent at home while the political leaders promote their own ideologies of national security and unquestioning patriotism as adjunct to their plans for militaristic conquest abroad. It is no wonder that the opening words of one of Bonhoeffer's early talks to his colleagues in the ecumenical movement were his claim that "the church is dead." By that he meant that the churches by their silence in the immorality of war were denying their own calling to represent Jesus Christ to the world especially in times of turmoil. "The church renounces obedience [to Christ] should it sanction war. The church of Christ stands against war for peace among people, between nations, classes and races."[50]

The Hiddenness of Prayer and of the Practice of Piety

In this section of Bonhoeffer' *Discipleship* he develops the correlative that the Christian life's "hiddenness" as such is made possible by the hiddenness of genuine Christian prayer. In the Christian community, disciples pray through Jesus Christ

49. D (DBWE 4), 152.

50. TF, 104.

their mediator. As with Jesus, so with Christians, trust has to exist "that God knows what we need before we ask for it."[51] The answer to such prayer depends neither on set formulae, that one can find in any stock of prayer books, nor on the proliferation of words but only through childlike faith. This must be, as Bonhoeffer insists, a hidden act in which the person of prayer communes with God without the fanfare of the public prayers that, as he observed in the parishes of Nazi Germany, could easily degenerate into "empty phrases."[52]

Bonhoeffer is also aware that private prayers too can deteriorate into merely listening to oneself, at times in exasperation at God's delay in responding with some sign that the prayer is heard. God, he says, is not fooled at such turning in on oneself. Hence his question on the need always to be on guard against such a deception: "How can I protect myself from myself?"[53] His reply is to allow Jesus' will alone to reign in one's heart. At this juncture and by way of illustrating the nature of a hidden prayer, he takes his readers through the various petitions of Jesus' own prayer. Of these, perhaps the most remarkable in the historical context of an anti-Christian ideology seeping into Christian consciousness and supplanting their allegiance to Jesus Christ is the petition for God's Kingdom to come. "This is where Satan is overcome, the power of the world, sin, and death broken. God's kingdom still is found in suffering and in struggle. The small community of those called forth will participate in such suffering and struggle. They stand under the rule of God in new righteous-

51. D (DBWE 4), 153.
52. D (DBWE 4), 153.
53. D (DBWE 4), 154.

ness, but also in enduring persecution."[54] God's Kingdom and God's will for the Christian community, Bonhoeffer concludes, must dominate even as the needs, both public and private, both urgent and long range, are expressed. Throughout this entire section on the hiddenness of prayer we can see Bonhoeffer's concern that prayer itself could be used, as it was, as a public display of church acquiescence in a leader who speaks as if he were himself a person of prayer and thus be blessed by God, though the Christian community find in such a leader only hypocrisy and duplicity.

Bonhoeffer adds that Jesus expects his followers to practice forms of austerity by way of disciplining their own will, too easily prone to selfishness and lethargy. Without such discipline, a would-be disciple would be unfit for the self-denial and self-sacrifice demanded by Jesus Christ of his followers. Bonhoeffer recalls Jesus' own warnings about the weakness of the flesh despite the human spirit's willingness. An example he invokes is the possible acceptance by the spirit of Jesus' command to forgive enemies even while that acceptance might be rejected by the "flesh" as too difficult. Daily prayer and especially daily meditation on God's word are the primary, disciplinary help in the flesh's tug of war against the spirit. Bonhoeffer counsels his readers not to lose sight of the fact that their daily life in fidelity to Jesus Christ is alien to the world that worships the ersatz gods of a secularized society. According to Bonhoeffer, Christians must ready themselves to undertake service in the cause of peace and justice through practices of discipline that include both fasting and prayer.[55]

54. D (DBWE 4), 156.
55. D (DBWE 4), 160.

Even here, however, Bonhoeffer warns against subtle attempts to replace Christ's sufferings with one's own attention-gathering public asceticism. Christians might be tempted to try to outdo Jesus Christ himself through some ostentatious show in one's highly public endurance of bodily suffering. Bonhoeffer contends that followers of Christ need hiddenness and considerable humility that looks to please Christ alone in serving God and not use their deeds, even in helping others, as an opportunity to be admired and lauded for such service. They needed to do the service for Christ alone and to keep Christ always in view. Daily meditation held the key for him in his efforts to please none other than Jesus Christ. Hence his advice to his seminarians, stuck in harm's way on the battlefields on the eastern front, is apropos his insistence on the daily discipline of meditation in order to keep their bearings in the midst of the public denial of Jesus Christ in the killing fields of World War II. Of all the "asceticisms" and disciplines Bonhoeffer recommends, daily meditation is above them all if the focus is to remain on Jesus Christ and not on oneself. In Bonhoeffer's words from a circular letter to his former seminarians, most of whom would not survive the war: "Daily, quiet attention to the Word of God which is meant for me, even if it is only for a few minutes, will become for me the focal point of everything which brings inward and outward order into my life. In the interruption and fragmentation of our previous ordered life, which in these days has been disrupted and broken up, and we are in danger of losing inner discipline through the host of events, the incessant claims of work and service, through doubt and temptation, struggle and disquiet of all kinds, meditation gives our life something like constancy, it keeps the link with our previous life, from baptism to confirmation, to ordination. It keeps us in the saving fellowship of the community, the brethren, our spiritual home."[56]

SIMPLICITY OF THE CAREFREE LIFE

Commenting on the Matthean gospel where Jesus tells his followers they cannot serve two masters (Matt 6:19–24), Bonhoeffer returns to his earlier emphasis on following Christ with one's heart totally given over to Jesus Christ alone. One cannot cling to the deceptive enticements of the world that can darken the heart and block the word of God from ever entering into the mind and affections of the disciple. Bonhoeffer does not denounce the use of the goods of the earth, but he does caution against the way disciples could be tempted to amass those goods like a hoarded treasure to which those who declare themselves followers of Christ might attach themselves. He excoriates the cleverness of those Christians and their churches that have so uncritically declared the compatibility of their accumulation of excessive wealth with God's approval. Their separation of the riches, which they say are essential to their ministry or the business aspect of their secular lives, from the cautionary mandate of Jesus Christ to beware of serving two masters is thus ignored and they become unwilling either to criticize or to counteract political, corporate or personal greed in their daily lives.

For Bonhoeffer, however, such a tactic is nothing more than self-deception. One cannot be a disciple and live with a divided heart. It would be a contradiction of Jesus who tells his followers they can have only one master. One must choose

56. TF, 457; translation slightly altered.

between God and allegiance to the world. Bonhoeffer uses strong language here in showing how love of the world can turn one's proclaimed love of God into actual hatred that, in effect, withdraws one's heart from communion with Jesus Christ.[57] This entire section of *Discipleship* would be echoed in Bonhoeffer's *Ethics* where he denounces the "thinking in two spheres" mentality in which Christians were encouraged to separate their secular, profane, and "unchristian" aspects of their lives from the sphere that belonged properly to their church activities and religious practice or even faith itself. The attempt to stand in both spheres, he claims, dooms the disciples to eternal conflict.

Conceding that it is difficult to break the spell of so-called Christians living in those two contradictory spheres, Bonhoeffer nonetheless argues that the attitude "is in profound contradiction to the thought of the Bible and to the thought of the Reformation. . . . There are not two realities, but only one reality, and that is the reality of God which has become manifest in Christ in the reality of the world. Sharing in Christ we stand at once in both the reality of God and the reality of the world. The reality of Christ comprises the reality of the world within itself."[58] His argument is remarkable in the simplicity of its Christocentrism. He recognizes the danger posed by abandonment of Christ's vision for the world and the manner in which even basically good people can succumb to the temptations to fall into the compromises in morality for which worldly attitudes are particularly prone, business and government plaudits given to acts of avarice and

57. D (DBWE 4), 162–64.

58. E (DBWE 6), 197.

violence serving as prime examples of why it is necessary to be single-minded in following Christ.

The great benefit of this simplicity is, as Bonhoeffer goes on to advocate, the elimination of the worry that causes people to fret about tomorrow's problems, today's needs for worldly goods, and amassing treasures as totems of personal success. These anxieties bind the disciples in chains of insecurity. Yet, with the gift of Jesus Christ that they have all received, Christians should have unconditional confidence in the protection and care of their Lord. Bonhoeffer reiterates what he has read in Paul who in his letter to the Romans asks his readers to trust that God will give them everything else that they as followers of Jesus Christ could ever need (Rom 8:32). Bonhoeffer claims that here one finds a source of the great liberation that takes place when one ceases to worry about the future, which is beyond human control, but learns to place that future in the hands of God. He goes on to say that such worry is what one expects to find among nonbelievers who, in the absence of God in their lives, are forced to rely solely on their own abilities and physical strength for the fulfillment of their needs. For Bonhoeffer, "communion with Jesus and obedience to his commandment come first; then everything else follows."[59] He closes with the observation that those who have followed Jesus Christ for a long time would be able to answer the related question: "How could they suffer need who in hunger and nakedness, persecution and danger are confident of their community with Jesus Christ?"[60]

59. D (DBWE 4), 167.
60. D (DBWE 4), 168.

The Community of Disciples as Set Apart and the Messengers

In these concluding sections of the first part of *Discipleship*, Bonhoeffer turns to the question of the relationship between the followers of Jesus Christ and the people, many of them nonbelievers and even enemies of those who have answered the call of Jesus in faith and full commitment. He asks if the followers of Christ have been made special with full authority over others to go along with their unique gifts. Indeed, Bonhoeffer acknowledges that such a misunderstanding of the special nature of Christian faith has existed in periods of religious history and can still be detected in some churches that do operate under authoritarian structures. He claims that the destructive, judgmental attitudes that had prevailed were traceable to a fracture of the bond that connects disciples to Jesus Christ. The mischief entered into Christian history when the disciples thought themselves the "measuring standard" for judging righteousness and they, not Jesus, were the center of the Christian church-community. When Jesus becomes the only center and exemplar of righteousness, then the disciples of Christ are empowered to approach others, like Jesus, with love and community.[61]

According to Bonhoeffer, the disciples' proper encounter with other people should become in turn, not their control over the lives of others, but the claim others make on their love and service. In this perspective, Jesus' unconditional love for the sinner is the standard of the Christian community's behavior toward nonbelievers and even enemies; sinners are loved but their sins condemned, not with cruel sanctions, but

61. See D (DBWE 4), 170–71.

by the very love of Christ that overcomes all evil. The difference is bound up in the sufferings of Jesus Christ that bestows forgiveness and obviates the caustic judgments against sinners that can blind disciples to their own sins and tear a community apart. The context of Bonhoeffer's words here lies in the seeming triumph of evil in the Nazi era and the inability of believers like Bonhoeffer and his colleagues in the Confessing Church to do much to oppose it.[62]

Bonhoeffer sees a danger similar to the judgmentalism and the condemnations that could shred the ties of community in Jesus Christ, namely, proselytizing. Bonhoeffer calls "self-defeating" any efforts to force people into patterns of belief and behavior in conformity with one's own way of following Christ or following some secular lord. There are times, he says, when hearts are hardened and doors are locked against the truth. In such instances one has to accept that especially here there is a need for Christian forbearance. Bonhoeffer recognizes that a popular idea can appear to outweigh even the power of God's word in the popular imagination. Alluding to the powerful propaganda of Adolf Hitler and the Nazi ministry of propaganda, he conceded that "the witnesses to the word are weaker than the propagandists of an idea."[63]

Christians, he points out, are not called to turn God's word into a dominant idea. They may very well, despite their best efforts, be too weak and less than "effective" in preaching and making that word attractive to their enemies. In which case, they are called to suffer because of their own limitations and the seeming triumph of those who are apparently powerful enough to oppose and try to destroy the word of God in

62. D (DBWE 4), 171.

63. D (DBWE 4), 173.

Jesus Christ. Bonhoeffer is here counseling a realistic attitude on the part of those who follow Jesus Christ. The power of disciples is constricted; their only power lies in Christian communion with none other than Jesus Christ. Their efforts may terminate in failure, dejection, and suffering at the hands of those they know to be the enemies of the truth. Judgment and toughness in relating to others in various opposing camps is reserved to the toughness followers of Christ should exert on themselves, always aware, however, that their sins are forgiven in Jesus Christ and they live, not from increasing their numbers and the strength of their authority, but "solely from God's love."[64]

The Great Separation

Bonhoeffer understands that the call to discipleship also entails a powerful separation from those who do not heed Christ's call. Genuine followers of Christ are evidently destined to be only a minority within their nation and among the masses of people who prefer to follow the dictates of a powerful secular ruler or who are coerced by fear and threats of punishment within a police state. Bonhoeffer reminds his readers of the sobering reality that followers of Christ should never put their trust in numbers. He is emphatic in his warning against measuring the strength of a church-community by the number of those who fill the pews on Sunday or on the number of converts one can add to the parish membership. The pathway to eternal communion with Jesus Christ, he says, is very narrow and disciples can easily get lost. Taking the narrow road means that the disciples will have to distin-

64. D (DBWE 4), 175.

guish between the mere appearances of Christian faith or pseudo-Christianity and the reality of what following Christ more faithfully in true discipleship can demand in terms of one's actions.[65]

The separation Bonhoeffer describes goes deeper into the community where some might be able to call Jesus Lord out of hidden, distorted reasons apart from the guidance of God's Spirit. Here Bonhoeffer recalls Paul's contention that "no one can call Jesus Lord, except by the Holy Spirit" (1 Cor 12:3). According to Bonhoeffer, it takes more than human rationality to confess that aspect of one's faith. True followers of Christ should realize that such a confession is not in any way salvific. The measure of the truth of the confession of faith lies always in the actions done in faith that ensue or that precede the declaration that Jesus Christ is Lord of all. Words come easily when ulterior motives are present. The actions that are born out of the risk of suffering and death mark the truth of any creedal proclamation. Hence Bonhoeffer's comment: "God will not ask us someday whether our confession was evangelical but whether we did God's will."[66] In an earlier sermon, Bonhoeffer preached a similar word: "God will ask us solely about the everlasting gospel: Did you believe and obey the gospel? God won't ask whether we were Germans or Jews, whether we were Nazis or not, not even whether we belonged to the Confessing Church or not."[67] Bonhoeffer insists here that doing the will of God constitutes the only authentic test of the disciples' fidelity to Jesus' call.

65. D (DBWE 4), 177–78.

66. D (DBWE 4), 179.

67. TF, 265.

The "separation" on which Bonhoeffer is commenting in this section is that of confessors of faith in Jesus and that of doers of Jesus' commands. Yet, even in this distinction Bonhoeffer notes the danger of doing the works of Christianity only in an effort at self-sanctification without love and without Christ and his Holy Spirit. To these Jesus can say, as he does in the gospel, he never knew them. The words of a confession can come easily enough, but to do the will of Christ can bring with the action a whole host of dangers. In every Christian work of love and service, the full focus once again must necessarily be on Jesus Christ who, in intimate communion with the disciple actually does the graced deed. This alone merits what Bonhoeffer concludes will be the great word at the disciple's entrance into eternal communion with Jesus Christ: "I have known you."[68]

The Messengers, Their Work and Their Suffering

Chapter 7 constitutes Bonhoeffer's final section of the first part of *Discipleship*. He calls his commentary "An Interpretation of Matthew 10" and begins with an examination of Jesus' plea for prayers that more laborers can be sent for the harvest which is quite simply too great and vast for the limited number of his followers. Bonhoeffer begins with a focus on Jesus taking pity on the people. Meeting their many needs had become a source of sadness to Jesus, especially when it seemed at the same time his disciples were attempting to keep Jesus isolated from the crowds that included bothersome children and importuning beggars. Jesus, in turn, would not permit the dis-

68. D (DBWE 4), 180.

ciples to limit his ministry to the inner circle he had called at the onset of his ministry. In so limiting the outreach of God's word, the disciples were unwittingly denying the people the protection and nourishment any flock of sheep would require. They were not like the good shepherd of Jesus' own analogy.[69] It is clear that Bonhoeffer is applying God's word in Jesus' gospel teachings on properly shepherding the flock to his own people under the Hitler dictatorship. In each instance the people have questions but are left without answers; they have needs but receive no help; they have their consciences frozen in fear but experience no freedom; they have tears but are given no consolation. In sum, the flock that Jesus grieves over has its counterpart in the Christians of Nazi Germany who experience a misuse of God's word. A revealing footnote to this passage states that the Nazi Bishop, Ludwig Müller is cited as having boasted of *Germanizing* the Sermon on the Mount in a not so well veiled attempt to eliminate the Jewish content.[70]

In Nazi Germany Bonhoeffer lamented the absence of good pastors for the church communities. Instead, he saw too many of those who neglected their people or who ruled with authoritarian violence while looking after their own personal needs. One of his complaints in the form of a question born of frustration must have hit home with the academicians, bishops, and preachers during the fear-laden Hitler years. "What did it matter that the most orthodox preachers and interpreters of the word of God were present, if they were not filled with all of the mercy and all of the grief over the abused and ill-treated people of God? What use are scholars

69. D (DBWE 4), 184.

70. D (DBWE 4), 184.

of Scripture, pious followers of the law, preachers of the word, if the shepherds of the church-community themselves are missing?"[71]

The Apostles and Their Work

In his description of the apostles or messengers who were the first sent to the "harvest" and who first formed the answer to Jesus' prayer for laborers, Bonhoeffer emphasizes their being gifted by Jesus with power. He is speaking of the power that made them effective against the machinations of the devil's own counterforce. In a sense Bonhoeffer associates this bestowal of power with Jesus' own ability to overcome and drive out evil spirits. He concludes that the call of Christ is the only detectable unifying force that could take twelve disparate followers, overcome their divisions, and use them to found a strong community of his followers to undertake and continue his mission.

That work, as Bonhoeffer continues to address the call to discipleship, parallels the commission to go "to the lost sheep of the house of Israel" (Matt 10:5–6). What is clear from Jesus' words, as quoted by Bonhoeffer, is that the followers of Christ are not free to choose where they are to work. They follow, not their own inclinations, affections, or interests but where they are sent. Their call is particularized by the command of Jesus in the power of God's word. A note in the text argues that the context of this focus on the "house of Israel" is the claim of the nazified Reich Church leaders that they should reach out

71. D (DBWE 4), 184–85.

only to their fellow Germans and not to the "thousand Jewish Christians."[72]

According to Bonhoeffer, followers of Christ are sent; they are not out on their own whim. They preach and the work they do differs little from Christ's original mandate. They preach the Kingdom of God, to be sure, but in the process of establishing Christian communities they also heal the sick, cleanse lepers, raise the dead, and cast out demons. Bonhoeffer notes also that the original followers are conscious that their power is, in reality, that of God's creative, redemptive word in Jesus Christ. But their credibility with the people is reinforced by their poverty, the absence of prestige or official power. Their effectiveness is not tied to their educational background, intellectual brilliance, or social standing, even if they are later confirmed as pastor. They also do their work without payment. They must be free from the ties of property and they must not parade themselves as deserving of honors. Any honor belongs to Jesus Christ alone who sends them and empowers them to preach the word and continue Christ's ministry.[73]

In this entire section one can only wonder whether Bonhoeffer was not engaged in stating a contrast between Jesus' directives and the practices of clericalized churches that had sunk in their credibility and influence because of the affluence they enjoyed. One can wonder too about the many honors, privileges, and perquisites bestowed on those who were the leaders of the established churches, most of whom were loyal to Adolf Hitler in that troubled era of German history. It is apropos to recall a statement attributed to Hitler

72. D (DBWE 4), 188.

73. D (DBWE 4), 186–87.

and contained in a small collection of what was purported to be Hitler's table talk. Hitler tells a fellow Nazi leader not to worry about any dangerous or powerful opposition from the churches. "Don't worry about the churches. I have them in my back pocket. I pay their salaries." Bonhoeffer concludes that their ministry is likewise a struggle against Satan for the hearts and souls of the people. The seriousness of the disciples' work is seen in Bonhoeffer's identifying their task as a struggle with Satan. He calls this a "struggle for the hearts of the people, this renunciation of their own reputation, possessions, and joys of the world, for the sake of serving the poor, the mistreated, and the miserable."[74]

The Suffering of the Messengers

By the very fact of their being sent by Jesus, Bonhoeffer notes in remarking on the courage needed by Jesus' followers that they do, indeed, receive the Lord's promise to be with them at every stage of their ministry, including their moments of suffering. This presence is a constant when the disciples are beset by apparent failure and the enmity of powerful political and religious leaders. If they are themselves defenseless, full of fear, and in danger, they can, nonetheless, count on Jesus' being present in and with them and his Spirit gives them what to say when brought to judgment. Even here, however, Bonhoeffer indicates the possibility of misinterpreting Jesus' teaching the disciples through the metaphors of being wise as a serpent and as simple as a dove. He states that the disciples must not try to avoid suffering by serpentine tricks of worldly cleverness. The disciple should also distinguish between suf-

74. D (DBWE 4), 190.

fering freely accepted in communion with Jesus Christ and sheer recklessness. The key to achieving a balance between the metaphors lies always in the word of God where the disciples can discover true wisdom and true simplicity.[75]

This word, Bonhoeffer continues, confers on the disciple a useful knowledge of the people among whom the disciples have their ministry. Although they should not show fear or mistrust, given the dangers they must face, neither should they give in to hatred of their obvious enemies or fall into the naiveté that exposes the disciple to greater danger under the false assumption that all people are good. Without a sense of the realism of their calling, they might be overwhelmed by the hatred and false accusations that can only intensify their suffering. Bonhoeffer adds that, in the midst of their troubles, they have the opportunity to become the good news that "will be propagated by suffering. That is the plan of God and the will of Jesus; and that is why in the hour of accountability before courts and thrones the disciples will be given the power to give a good confession, to offer a fearless witness. The Holy Spirit will be with them. It will make them invincible."[76]

According to Bonhoeffer, the one great consolation the disciples have in the midst of their sufferings is that they thereby remain in communion with the cross of Jesus Christ. The witness the disciples give in their sufferings when fear can beset them is their confidence that the torments they may face will be revealed publicly as a judgment against their persecutors. The gospel must be made public and not shrink into what Bonhoeffer denounces as "a sectarian affair."[77]

75. D (DBWE 4), 193.
76. D (DBWE 4), 194.
77. D (DBWE 4), 196.

Bonhoeffer tells his readers that the public witness by followers of Christ should not be stymied by fear of their enemies. The powers of hatred and the sufferings inflicted by enemies of Christ and the gospel stop with their violent, physical death, but that time is short compared to eternity. Bonhoeffer offers this consolation to those who experience fear, rejection, violence, and even death itself in their ministry to a people whose hearts have been hardened against them. "Those who remain faithful to the word and the confession here will find that Jesus Christ will stand by them in the hour of judgment. . . . Those who have held on to Jesus in this life will find that Jesus will hold on to them in eternity."[78] The courage that Bonhoeffer himself showed at the moment of his own execution undoubtedly can be traced to his attitude expressed here toward the inevitable suffering inflicted on those involved like him in a dangerous mission; in his case to bring an end to a world war and the genocidal death camps.

Part Two: The Church of Jesus Christ and Discipleship

Preliminary Questions

Bonhoeffer's preliminary questions deal with how Jesus' call to his followers when he was visibly present can still reach present day disciples. He dismisses the attempts to differentiate between the call of a physically visible Jesus back then and the problem of discerning the call in the palpable absence of Jesus Christ in the world of Bonhoeffer's struggle against Nazism. He contends, rather, that Jesus is not dead but by

78. D (DBWE 4), 197.

his resurrection still alive and recognized by faith, though not by sight. Jesus continues to speak his scriptural word and call disciples to follow him. That presence is recognized in all ages within the church-community in God's word and the sacraments. One listens to the gospel and encounters Christ afresh, "already present as the glorified, the victorious, the living Christ."[79] This Christ, Bonhoeffer argues, still calls disciples to follow him by their faith today just as back in his public life. In any given time frame, those called to undertake the same mission of Jesus Christ begin, like the first disciples, by having faith in Christ's word. It is the same Christ who calls to discipleship and the same dynamic grace of faith that impels the disciple to follow. Affirming Christ's presence and the contemporary call is important to Bonhoeffer because of the widespread attitude that Christ and his teachings had lost their relevance in their modern age when the realities of war and patriotism seemed to exclude Jesus Christ from political decision making. In his denunciations of war and the steps leading to war, Bonhoeffer often invoked the teachings of Jesus Christ as motivation for church leaders to become advocates for peace.

Another question raised by Bonhoeffer relates to whether the first followers of Christ were at an advantage. This, too, he rejects, arguing that it is the same Christ who in the present era speaks exactly as he did when he called the first followers. It is still Christ's word and command that enabled those disciples to recognize him as their Lord. For Bonhoeffer, the timeline of being encountered or called by Jesus Christ does not matter. Jesus' command transcends time in the singular-

79. D (DBWE 4), 202.

ity and uniqueness of his word, continually demanding "faith from an undivided heart and love of God and neighbor with all our heart and soul."[80] Bonhoeffer contends that invidious comparisons between the earliest disciples when Jesus was alive in his public life and those called to follow Christ in the later Hitler era or in any historical period pose a misleading alternative. It is the one Christ then as now. With that understanding, Bonhoeffer will proceed to relate the call to discipleship to where that call is heard and received in the church-community. In the ensuing sections he addresses Baptism, the mystical Body of Christ, the visible church-community and the Saints with the allied issues of sanctification and holiness.

Baptism and the Death to One's Previous Life

In this second part of *Discipleship*, Bonhoeffer is eager to affirm the continuity between the synoptic vision of discipleship and the Pauline emphasis in the light of Jesus' never ending resurrection presence as the risen Lord. These are two perspectives, to be sure, but Paul only confirms the synoptic portrait and vice-versa. Paul's references depict Christ continuing to be present in ways no different from the synoptic Christ. The whole of Scripture, Bonhoeffer argues, attests to this continuity.[81] Having said that, Bonhoeffer goes on to indicate the different terminology and what that does to reinforce the synoptic call to discipleship. For Paul, baptism becomes the visible sign that the call to discipleship is answered. Paul speaks of a disciple being baptized into Christ and receiving

80. D (DBWE 4), 203.

81. D (DBWE 4), 205–6.

the grace to announce and effect a public break with the past. He proclaims that Christ makes the break possible. At baptism Christ steps between the disciples and their world. They can no longer belong to or serve the world. They are subject to Jesus Christ alone.[82] This is, to be sure, a spiritual death to oneself that is the prelude to the rise of the new self in the power of Christ's own death on the cross and resurrection into glory. In effect, Bonhoeffer recognizes that in the Pauline tradition baptism brings the disciple into a communion with Jesus Christ who gifts his followers with justification, forgiveness of their sins and a new life that includes death to the self and to one's sins past and present.[83]

What is more, Bonhoeffer relates baptism to the advent of God's Spirit in the hearts of those called through their acceptance of baptism to follow Jesus Christ. Here the ensuing acts of disciples emerge into the visibility of the church-community as the world and even family and possessions are given up. They now begin their life in the cross of Christ, source of the inner graced strength to abandon the attractions of their previous life and to enjoy the new life that communion with Jesus Christ makes both possible and attractive.[84]

THE BODY OF CHRIST

Once again, Bonhoeffer links the bodily community of Jesus and the earlier gospel portrait of Jesus and the apostles with the church-community of the present era. It is the same "full

82. D (DBWE 4), 208.
83. D (DBWE 4), 209.
84. D (DBWE 4), 211–12.

community with the bodily presence of the glorified Lord."[85] The great miracle of God's becoming a human being meant that God sent the son in the flesh that Jesus Christ might bear the full weight of humanity as a whole. Bonhoeffer sees this amazing transformation in which Jesus Christ as an individual is at the same time the "new humanity" doing everything on behalf of his bodily communion with his disciples. In this bodily communion Jesus proclaims his genuine need for a community of followers. While Jesus carried his disciples to the cross, he also brought them into his resurrection life in the Spirit where the signs of his communion with them, baptism and the Lord's supper, continue to keep his presence alive in their hearts and in their actions for others. In these sacraments, Bonhoeffer points out that followers of Christ are reminded that they live in the present with and in Christ, never to lose sight of the new reality that "Christ is in us."[86]

The church-community, in this Pauline perspective, thus becomes through baptism into Christ a body that is Christ's own physical and spiritual presence with his followers in every age of Christian history. According to Bonhoeffer, Christ lives "for us" in word, attitude and even in bodily life when Christ is recognized in oneself and in others. Here Bonhoeffer identifies the body of Christ closely with the church-community to the point that, for him, "to be in Christ means to be in the church-community." He goes so far as to declare that "the church is the present Christ himself."[87] He says this, he admits, to get his readers away from thinking of the church as an institution instead of as a person in that unique sense

85. D (DBWE 4), 213.

86. D (DBWE 4), 216.

87. D (DBWE 4), 218.

of which Christ is a person. With Kierkegaard Bonhoeffer can affirm that Christianity is not a doctrine but a person to whom we entrust ourselves irrevocably.[88]

At this juncture Bonhoeffer focuses on the Pauline description of baptism and life in the church-community as a "putting on" of Christ, adding that this Jesus is neither Jew nor Greek, neither slave or free person, beyond class or ethnic distinctions but faithful to all those who belong to him. Having affirmed the work of the Holy Spirit in creating the church-community in Christ's body, Bonhoeffer also argues for the oneness of that body even in the amazing plurality of the far-flung membership. The upshot of the Spirit's power in shaping this body is that disciples "no longer live our own lives, but Christ lives in us."[89] This is close to Augustine's surprising realization that God is "more intimate to me that I am to myself."[90]

Such intimacy implies further that disciples must be willing to take part in the cross of Christ. Bonhoeffer calls this sharing in Christ's sufferings an "immeasurable grace to suffer 'for him.'"[91] He makes it clear that such suffering in the power of Christ's own body is a vicarious action that benefits the church-community itself and in its specific mission. His sentiments here will dovetail with his remarkable statement in his letters from prison: "By this worldliness I mean living unreservedly in life's duties, problems, successes and failures, experiences and perplexities. In so doing we throw ourselves completely into the arms of God, taking seriously, not our

88. See Dupré, *Kierkegaard as Theologian*, 137.

89. D (DBWE 4), 221.

90. Augustine, *Confessions*, 3.6.11 (Boulding, 44).

91. D (DBWE 4), 221.

own sufferings, but those of God in the world."[92] Later in his letters he will state that only a God who suffers can help Christians in their time of crisis. He concludes this segment of *Discipleship* with additional praise for the value of suffering which he calls both a gift and a privilege. In his view, God gives to some the grace and privilege to suffer for the body of Christ and such suffering, as Paul has taught, can become a source of joy (Phil 2:17). In the Pauline image of the Body of Christ, Bonhoeffer concludes that the church in communion with Jesus Christ and the first disciples is "the place where God is truly and bodily present. . . . The body of Christ is thus the place of acceptance, the place of reconciliation and of peace between God and human beings."[93]

The Visible Church-Community

Just as Christ is God become incarnate and highly visible on earth, so too Bonhoeffer argues that the church-community needs its own visibility to accomplish its mission among peoples. Jesus, he says, does not rely on doctrines or authoritarian structures to teach; but he does need actual human beings to be his followers and to continue his mission on earth. Hence in his earlier description of Jesus' sermon on the mount, he alluded to the call for disciples to be a light for the world or like a city seated on a mountain top. The followers of Jesus in a church-community are the embodiment of Jesus' acts and sufferings. Bonhoeffer sees this visibility in the preaching of the word and the teaching of the apostles who witnessed to the resurrection. According to Bonhoeffer, the word of God

92. LPP, 370.

93. D (DBWE 4), 224.

necessarily seeks out community where the word can be heard and witnessed. The apostles did, in fact, bear witness to the word become flesh to forgive sins and sanctify the disciples now ensconced in a church-community bearing his name.[94] It is the same word that brings the church-community into being through baptism and the Lord's Supper.

Bonhoeffer notes further that this communion in Christ's body involves both differentiation in its membership and a common order that emphasizes service through love and compassion in ministries under the guidance of the Holy Spirit.[95] At this point Bonhoeffer lists the servants of the church-community from apostles, prophets, teachers, overseers, deacons, elders, presiding officers, and leaders, all contributing in their own way to the body of Jesus Christ. Even as the order and those servants are recognized for their service, Bonhoeffer cautions against the possibility of deviation from the gospel values into desires for worldly gain and acclaim. In his view, the temptation to bestow honors, to use power to dominate, or to increase wealth and physical comfort continues to threaten the churches. He recognizes also the possible slippage into incessant bickering over differences in theological interpretation, some of which he had already seen in his own theological training at Berlin University where it was difficult at times to distinguish between theology and heresy. He adds that, once the heresy is recognized as such, it has to be rejected, an obvious reference to his own insistence that the Reich Church, with its emphasis on loyalty to Adolf Hitler and its reliance on the Nazi ideology in its church directives,

94. D (DBWE 4), 227–28.

95. D (DBWE 4), 230.

was in heresy and, thereby, should be condemned for its pollution of the Christian gospel.

Bonhoeffer then turns again to the need for a church-community to have sufficient living space in order to live out its commitment to Jesus Christ. To illustrate this he invokes the Lukan attestation of the public witness of the earliest church-community to the presence of Jesus' teachings put into practice in Acts 2:4. That community held all things in common; it kept the material needs and use of material goods in proper perspective through sharing; it enjoyed a freedom grounded in the gospel; it knew its place in God's Kingdom through preaching the word and celebrating the sacrament of the Lord's Supper. He concludes with the overall effect on the attractiveness of this early community. Its members were "of one heart and soul" (Acts 4:32).

Bonhoeffer points out that such a visible church-community cannot help but grow in numbers through the power of its witness to the life, death, and resurrection of Jesus Christ but also through the impulse of the Holy Spirit. The increase in membership is described in the passages cited above. Bonhoeffer connects this spectacular growth to the original witness and the attraction of Jesus' presence as word and sacrament. In a way, he views this growth as sign that, in a good sense, the church-community has "invaded the world and captivated its children."[96]

Bonhoeffer goes on to argue that there is more to the church-community than the gifts of baptism and the Lord's Supper. He turns to the problem of human relationships as these affect life in the community. From personal experi-

96. D (DBWE 4), 233.

ence, he knows of the racial problems within his own country and of the natural antipathies that can erode the spirit of the church-community. In an earlier catechetical lesson he had declared that "Within the church-community there is neither . . . Jew nor German." He denounced the Nuremberg Laws of 1935 that "legalized" the overt prejudice against the Jews of Germany, including baptized Jews. Where such racism infiltrates the church-community Bonhoeffer calls this a profanation of the sacrament of baptism.[97] He uses the example of Paul's intervention on behalf of the runaway slave, Onesimus, to argue that the free master and the slave are equal members of the Christian church-community to the extent that followers of Jesus Christ are not to see people as free or slave, as man or woman, but they are to see all as members of Jesus' mystical body. In the historical context of Bonhoeffer's *Discipleship*, Onesimus stands for the beleaguered Jew of Nazi Germany.

Bonhoeffer continues to insist that this refusal to accept the social prejudices of the world is one important way in which the church-community impacts the world in its efforts to win space for Jesus Christ and the gospel teachings. The church-community refuses consent to any restrictions in its efforts to extend love and compassion to those made to suffer in civil society. His statement here is remarkable for its forthrightness and courage. "Where the world despises other members of the Christian family, Christians will love and serve them. If the world does violence to them, Christians will help them and provide them relief. Where the world subjects them to dishonor and insult, Christians will sacrifice their own honor in exchange for their disgrace."[98] Bonhoeffer

97. D (DBWE 4), 234–35.
98. D (DBWE 4), 237.

extended this solidarity to the church's obligation to protect and aid the Jews of Nazi Germany. He would frequently cite Proverbs 31:8 ("Speak out for those who have no voice") to justify his demand that the church speak out against the actions of the Nazi state in its vicious persecution of the Jews.

It should be obvious from this section of *Discipleship* that Bonhoeffer does not advocate a flight from the world, despite his arguments for a separation from the values that the world espouses. He goes so far as to declare a "frontal assault" on the world through the witness of the church-community to the dangers of the evils and ills advocated by worldly powers in decisions and actions that demean human beings. The motivation of the church-community is always Jesus Christ incarnate. The church-community witnesses to Jesus' own humanity as a human being who was executed by and in the midst of his enemies. Followers of Christ are to live like him in the world even as they fight against the coveted things of the world. Here Bonhoeffer recalls the example of Martin Luther who left the monastery, not to enjoy the enticements of the world, but to turn attitudes toward separation from the world and engagement with the world upside down. His return to the world was, in effect, a major step toward a protest against and a criticism of the godless secularization into which the so-called Christian world had fallen. Christians are to die to the world in the midst of the world, not safely ensconced in isolation from the world.[99] He adds that this combat is also revelatory of certain professions that are inimical for Christianity. In Nazi Germany, the prevailing ideology held the inverse of that assertion, namely, that being a good Nazi

99. D (DBWE 4), 244–45.

meant that certain professions were outlawed and legal measures were taken against those belonging to such. Teachers, catechists, lawyers who defended dissenters, and so on, were targeted. The danger, Bonhoeffer points out, could reach the point where the anti-Christian world would feel "compelled to force Christians to deny their Lord in exchange for every piece of bread they want to eat. In the end, Christians are thus left with no other choices except to escape from the world or to go to prison."[100] This statement in 1937 would become biographical for Bonhoeffer in his decision to leave Germany in the summer of 1939 only to return after one month to join the German resistance to Hitler until his arrest and imprisonment in 1943.[101]

Bonhoeffer concludes the section with his impression that the sacrifices of the Christians in their solidarity with the cross of Jesus Christ are the reasons why God preserves the world despite its notorious infidelities. Hence his belief that, though "Christians are poor and suffering, hungry and thirsty, gentle, compassionate and peaceable, persecuted and scorned by the world, . . . they suffer so that the world can still live under God's forbearance." The followers of Christ continue to die daily to the "old self" and give public witness to their dying to and often at the hands of the world. They become witnesses to the power of Christ's bodily and spiritual presence. In their faith they are determined to live as Christ did, even to the sacrifice of their own lives that the victims of societal oppression might be delivered and the world continue to live under the graced presence of God in Jesus Christ and in their spirit of love and compassion.

100. D (DBWE 4), 247.

101. D (DBWE 4), 251.

The Saints and Sanctification

Bonhoeffer states at the outset of this section that the goal of following Jesus Christ is to be holy and blameless before God. In this, he notes the separation that must always be kept in mind. "God alone is holy." Just as Jesus Christ is himself separated from the world of sin, his body is the realm of God's holiness extended to the world in God's becoming human in Jesus, thus carrying human beings themselves into his death on the cross. Bonhoeffer waxes poetic in this section, stating in metaphorical terms that, in a certain sense, God "kills" both his son Jesus and, in Jesus, us who, as disciples, take part in Jesus' life and death. At this apex point of God's incarnate life in Jesus Christ God's own righteousness is extended to the world of human beings in that sinners can now receive God's own righteousness, not as a personal possession, but as those justified, made righteous in the sight of God. In the death of Jesus Christ God's righteousness is now given to sinners who thereby become justified and open to the call to holiness through following in the pathways of God's own son Jesus Christ. The righteousness in question is not that of those called from sin to God's own life but that of Jesus Christ whose presence in and for us through his Holy Spirit has led us to a new life and a new presence in the world. In that sense, Bonhoeffer says that followers of Christ are in the communion of saints and can indeed be called saints.[102]

Following this theological analysis, Bonhoeffer turns his attention to the issue of the sanctification or holiness made possible and expected of the followers of Jesus Christ. If the sinners are now justified by God's grace, they are at the same

102. See D (DBWE 4), 253–59.

time preserved by God's continued graciousness for the demanding process of sanctification. This sanctification, Bonhoeffer says, keeps the disciples in the church-community where the separation from the world is made possible in anticipation of the end time. Bonhoeffer lists characteristics of the lifelong process of holiness. First, there is the visibility of discipleship in the church-community. There is also, secondarily, an involvement in the "political ethics" of the church-community in which God's word in Jesus Christ is proclaimed and the claim made that the earth is the Lord's.[103] Bonhoeffer recognizes that this attitude can place the church-community on a collision course with the world in which followers of Christ and their church-communities must struggle for the recognition and creation of God's realm on earth. The disciples are called to be holy in the midst of the "terribly dark" works perpetrated by evil forces in the world listed by Bonhoeffer citing Paul's catalogue of vices in Gal 5:19–21.[104]

Bonhoeffer claims further that being in the church-community with the body of Jesus Christ, at once transfigured and transformed, makes possible liberation from the disorderliness that is so rampant in the world. Against the realm of unchristian permissiveness where uncontrolled passions find expression in sins of the flesh, greed, and attitudes destructive of marriage, Bonhoeffer is able to invoke the Pauline condemnations and warnings that the perpetrators of such self-indulgence "have no part in the body of Christ."[105] Bonhoeffer is equally emphatic that the process of sanctification is a hidden accomplishment of God's Holy Spirit

103. See D (DBWE 4), 261–62.

104. See D (DBWE 4), 263–64.

105. D (DBWE 4), 266.

eliciting, not pride, but humility and gratitude. Here again, the visibility of the church-community remains the dynamic that offers a powerful witness to the power of the Spirit in the church-community impelling the world to concede that they too can see how followers of Christ do love one another.

Bonhoeffer gives another measure of the effectiveness of the church-community in showing itself worthy of Christ's gospel, namely, the God-given ability to forgive one another. In this, too, it is God who forgives and makes forgiveness of one another possible. The church-community, he insists, lives under God's forgiving compassion of which the practice of oral confession is both gift and symbol.[106] This forgiveness, Bonhoeffer adds, does not obviate the unpleasant task of the community to separate themselves from anyone whose sinful ways are judged to be not only incorrigible but also destructive of the community itself.

In describing a third hallmark of the process of sanctification within the church-community Bonhoeffer directs the reader's attention to the community's ability to "stand firm on the day of Jesus Christ." The language here becomes eschatological. Followers of Christ are to appear before him blameless and holy. Followers of Christ are to appear before him blameless and holy. Their judgment will be based on the good they have been mandated to do as disciples of Jesus Christ. By his graced presence Christ not only empowers goodness in his followers, he has also set before them the example of how faith is correlated with doing good to and for others. At a time when Christians were misinterpreting Luther to the effect that

106. See D (DBWE 4), 266–71; See also chapter 3 of this book for a more extensive explanation of the practice of oral confession in Bonhoeffer's seminary community. See also LT, 108–18.

good works were either useless for salvation or were merely "extras" that were easily "absolved" in favor of doing the bidding of a political dictator, Bonhoeffer's insistence on doing good is timely. In all his argument for the correct interpretation of Luther on this very point he is careful to give all credit to God in whom any good works "are nothing but God's own good works for which God has already prepared us."[107] Those works for sanctification and, only indirectly, for salvation, for which God must be given credit, are the same works that Jesus himself revealed when he identified with and begged for those experiencing hunger, thirst, nakedness, homelessness, and imprisonment to which the genuine followers of Christ, without always knowing the true source of their compassion, responded with characteristic generosity and love.[108]

THE IMAGE OF CHRIST

In his powerful concluding chapter Bonhoeffer sums up the call to discipleship as entering on a way of actually becoming like Jesus Christ. He insists that the followers of Christ must always keep the image of Jesus Christ before their eyes to the point that all other images are permeated and transformed by the power of Christ's image and presence. To be like Christ is in itself a process to be shaped in and through the church-community and the fostering of the gospel mandates to do as Christ did. In this connection Bonhoeffer recounts how the fall of Adam threw human nature into a mode of life bereft of God and by that tragic fact also bereft of human beings' basic humanity. No longer could the summit of God's

107. D (DBWE 4), 279.
108. D (DBWE 4), 279–80.

creation image the creator. Bonhoeffer goes on to describe the next stage in God's restoring humanity to its full potential. In that tragic moment of Adam's fall God began the process of reshaping the divine image in creation in the only perfect way possible, through the word of God fully enfleshed, like Adam, in human nature. The Son of God, Jesus Christ, in entering human history in solidarity with a specially selected people, became the "new Adam," taking on sinful human nature in the form of a servant for others (Phil 2:5).[109] According to Bonhoeffer, the incarnation of God's word in Jesus Christ was neither the advent of a new religion nor a new doctrinal idea. The new form was, rather, that of a warm-hearted, self-sacrificing, personable human being who arrived in the midst of a world in a turmoil not unlike the era in which Bonhoeffer was writing *Discipleship*. Bonhoeffer depicted Christ in his historical lifetime as a person "obedient to God's will in suffering and death; the one born in poverty, who befriended and sat at table to eat with tax collectors and sinners, and who, on the cross, was rejected and abandoned by God and human beings—this is God in human form, this is the human being who is the new image of God."[110]

Bonhoeffer calls the wounds of Jesus' sufferings the "signs of grace on the body of the risen and transfigured Christ." The cross dominates the image of Christ that Bonhoeffer wishes to associate in an essential way with the vocation of followers of Jesus Christ. The implications of this association are enormous for the entire thrust of the costly grace of Christian discipleship. The image of the suffering Christ, obedient unto death, is what pleases God the most and, at the same time,

109. See D (DBWE 4), 282–83.

110. D (DBWE 4), 284.

it is the image to which followers of Christ must conform themselves. This conformation and transformation is not something that disciples can accomplish on their own. It is, instead, the work of Christ himself who takes shape in every historical era in the church-community. The task of the disciples now is to bear that image and to be reshaped by Christ to the point that Christ be recognized in every human being now honored by God with the dignity of bearing the image of God's own Son. Here Bonhoeffer lashes out at the Nazi ideology that demeans individuals and groups of people whom Hitler and his minions had judged to be less than human (*Untermenschen*!). In a dramatic phrase that will in turn become a theme for his posthumously published, *Ethics*, he argues that "whoever from now on attacks the least of the people attacks Christ, who took on human form and who in himself has restored the image of God for all who bear a human countenance."[111] The reference to the persecuted Jewish people in Nazi Germany is unmistakable. In his *Ethics* he will ask the church to confess its complicity in the atrocities then being committed. The churches, he said, were "guilty of the lives of the weakest and most defenseless brothers and sisters of Jesus Christ."[112] Earlier, in an ecumenical sermon, he likened the killing of one another in war to a violence done to Jesus Christ by Christians who should know better.[113]

Bonhoeffer continues to speak in this chapter of how Christ himself becomes visible in and through the disciples who suffer public disgrace and even the degradation of being

111. D (DBWE 4), 285.

112. E (DBWE 6), 139. See also Clifford Green's perceptive critical commentary on this passage, 130–40.

113. TF, 228.

martyred for the sake of and in conformity with Jesus Christ. But these followers of Christ, having suffered and died, are likewise those who will be transformed into the image of the glorified Christ. The conformation to Jesus Christ is the graced effect of Christ's having dwelled in the hearts and souls of his followers to the point of Christ's continuing his earthly life and mission in the lives and actions for peace and justice of the disciples. In a sense Christian community life becomes, through imitating Jesus Christ, the actual embodiment of Jesus Christ such as Paul described in his claim that "it is no longer I who live, but it is Christ who lives in me" (Gal 2:20).[114]

Questions

1. Why does Bonhoeffer declare that cheap grace is the deadly enemy of the church? How does that contrast with costly grace? Are his statements true today?
2. What in your opinion is the danger of worldly attachments in following Jesus Christ? Is it possible to be possessed by one's possessions?
3. How does Bonhoeffer's statement, "Whenever Jesus calls us, his call leads us to death," apply to Christians today? Are there different forms in which such a "death" takes place?
4. How in your opinion can the Christian life of an individual lead to a severance of ties with one's family and nation? How would such "severance" square with the issue of loyalty to one's family and nation?

114. D (DBWE 4), 287–88.

5. Why does Bonhoeffer view the arms race and war in the name of national security as an "idolatry"? Is this "idol" still worshipped today in political circles?
6. What exactly does Bonhoeffer mean by his insistence on the credibility of the church in the face of systemic evil? What can be done to restore church credibility once it is lost?
7. What exactly, in Bonhoeffer's descriptions in his section on baptism, is abandoned and what is received at baptism? How effective is the baptismal ceremony in today's churches in instigating or renewing one's baptismal commitment to Jesus Christ?
8. Comment in terms of war, treatment of enemies in warfare, and racism in the United States, on Bonhoeffer's statement: "whoever from now on attacks the least of the people attacks Christ, who took on human form and who in himself has restored the image of God for all who bear a human countenance." (DBWE 4), 285.

THREE

Life Together: Bonhoeffer on Christian Community

Development of the Text

Bonhoeffer's Early Convictions on the Need for Community

We learn from Eberhard Bethge, Bonhoeffer's biographer, that, from his first days at Berlin University, Bonhoeffer had wanted to live in and help shape a Christian community.[1] He was intrigued with the problem of how to live out his profession of faith in Jesus Christ, both in his private life and in the church-community as well. His doctoral dissertation, *Sanctorum Communio*, attests to his inner longing for a community life in which his call to the Lutheran ministry and his love for God's word would give a more meaningful sense of direction to his life. Although Bonhoeffer had wanted for a long time to put into practice his desire to live in a genuine Christian community where the members would live together, share their concerns, and be committed to one another, the implementation of that desire first began to take concrete shape within the circle of some of his students. These were students who were drawn to his creative way of teaching the-

1. DB, 207–34.

ology and who saw themselves sharing his faith and Christian ideals. At Berlin University, his seminars, evening discussions, and country excursions brought him into closer contact with like-minded students, some of whom later became his colleagues in the church struggle. Several would enter the seminary to study under him.

Together with these students he organized frequent weekend trips to a rented cottage in the hilly countryside beyond the outskirts of Berlin where they could discuss theology, pray together, and enjoy long walks in the surrounding areas and listen to his collection of Black spirituals that he had brought back from his brief ministry at the Abyssinain Baptist Church in Harlem. Distancing themselves from the hubbub of university life, these young men were able to share thoughts on how to create Christian community through a combination of regular spiritual exercises and active work to help those in need. Those gatherings were informal and somewhat spontaneous, yet they provided some of the sparks for Bonhoeffer later to develop the kind of community life that he would incorporate into the seminary at Finkenwalde that he describes in his book, *Life Together.* By that time, he was anxious to use his experiences in community to reanimate the Christian churches in Germany, helping them to withstand the lure of Nazism.

In his lectures at the university, even before his experiences of community life at Finkenwalde, he was convinced that the church had to be thoroughly involved in and for the world of that time and not given to forms of ecclesiastical escapism from the problems of ordinary people. The Hitler era was forcing difficult choices on the citizens of Germany, while the main churches appeared to support the Nazi ideology that Bonhoeffer detested. He told his students that the church must never be reduced to a domesticated abstraction. He added that this church was subjected to all the weaknesses of the world. The church can, at times, like Christ himself, be "without a roof over its head." Further, its place in the world "consists in the church's being able to renounce all privileges and all its property but never Christ's Word and the forgiveness of sins. With Christ and the forgiveness of sins to fall back on, the church is free to give up everything else."[2] These words to his students in 1932 would find their echo in one of his last writings from prison, the "Outline for a Book" that promised to be a "Stocktaking of Christianity" with an exploration of "the real meaning of Christian faith."

There, in the last year of his life, he dared the church to be like Jesus Christ and to risk its very existence on serving those in need rather than in surrendering its integrity to some earthly dictator. The church, he wrote in that letter, should make a start by giving away "all its property to those in need."[3] The renunciation of privileges, the liberating word of Jesus Christ, and the forbearance needed to forgive sins would also be in the forefront of Bonhoeffer's concerns for his community of seminarians. His words on the self-sacrifices required by the churches continued to reverberate in his seminary lectures on following Jesus Christ, whom he regarded as the binding force that held the Christian community together in fidelity to the gospel and in mutual service to the word of God.

Most of Bonhoeffer's theological reflections on Christian community focused on the question of how God's gift of faith to individual believers assumes concrete form in a world of amazing diversity. He also pondered the question of how the

2. TF, 86–87; translation slightly altered.

3. LPP, 382.

individuals whose personalities shaped community life were able to undergo a growth in their spiritual strength through the sharing of their faith and their mutual service, all held together by their prayer life and mutual forbearance of one another. Faith in Jesus Christ, expressed through the bonding of Christians with each other, was more than a rationalized theory to Bonhoeffer. Hitler's popularity with the masses had generated a dilemma for the churches. Afraid to contradict what the people so enthusiastically praised in spite of their misgivings, most of the churches went along with the popular mood. Bonhoeffer became convinced that the failure of the churches to become prophetic communities in opposition to their government contributed to the perverse attractiveness of National Socialism with the majority of Germany's citizens. He criticized the churches for being turned in on themselves, stuck in their efforts to retain clerical privileges and perquisites, and lost in a kind of sanctimonious narcissism. Further, he lamented the obvious reality that the churches had, with disastrous consequences, failed to extend their compassionate outreach to those at the lowest level of German society.[4]

Earliest Writings on the Nature of Christian Community

It should come as no surprise that Bonhoeffer's writings on community converge in the person of Jesus Christ, whom he depicts as gracing people in their common humanity with dignity and a sense of purpose. He does not hesitate to claim that the moral demands of Jesus define all relationships. Bonhoeffer's unwavering Christocentrism moved him fur-

4. See CML, 148–49.

ther to assert that what may be the strength of all other forms of community becomes qualitatively different in communion with Jesus Christ within the Christian church-community. His most extensive study of the Christian church-community roams widely around his claims that human life itself can be fully understood only through one's social relations with others in those communities, which shape one's personal world of meaning. In like manner he sees God's revelation, the ultimate source of that meaning, reaching people only through their corporeal and social reality. In Jesus Christ, Bonhoeffer contends that God not only entered human history, but in a striking way God has directed that history by becoming inextricably bound up with human beings in all their concreteness. Jesus, in Bonhoeffer's theology of the "communion of saints," is the Lord through whom God's love, the foundation and binding force of all humanizing community, overcomes sin and brings about the reconciliation of individuals with themselves and with others, even sinners and enemies.[5] This is the immediate context for Bonhoeffer's claim that, to be truly the church, those who claim to follow Jesus Christ must become themselves "Christ existing as the church-community."[6]

Bonhoeffer writes glowingly of Christ's vicarious action as the soul of that community of disciples whose oneness would be structured by unconditional, other-centered love,

5. This summary analysis of Bonhoeffer's theology of the "communion of saints" is based on and developed more fully in two important texts. The first is his doctoral dissertation in the new translation and critical edition, *Sactorum Communio: A Theological Study of the Sociology of the Church*, edited by Clifford J. Green, volume 1 of the DBWE. The second is the superb analysis of Bonhoeffer's social theology by Clifford J. Green, *Bonhoeffer: A Theology of Sociality*.

6. SC (DBWE 1), 140–41.

their living and acting for others rather than for themselves. It is this self-sacrificing love that shapes the community into concrete resemblance to Jesus Christ. Bonhoeffer's distinction between being *with* and being *for* the others in community is apropos here. The churches of Germany, like so many churches in the United States today, were filled with parishioners who were merely occupying pews in proximity one to another; very few were there in any real sense to form a genuine community in love and service for the others. It has been said that in American churches, people come together without knowing each other, they live without loving each other, and they die without grieving for one another. A cynical statement, to be sure, but with an element of truth if the sole extent of parish life is simply to be bodily present during the Sunday services. For Bonhoeffer, the Christian community must proceed to the next stage, where the parishioners are there in order to be with Christ as they become Christ for others. He writes of that stage with an evident passion: "Whoever lives in love is Christ in relation to the neighbor. . . . Christians can and ought to act like Christ; ought to bear the burdens and sufferings of the neighbor. . . . It must come to the point that the weaknesses, needs, and sins of my neighbor afflict me as if they were my own, in the same way as Christ was afflicted by our sins."[7] His later statements on the necessity of forbearance in the church-community have their foundation in this powerful exhortation to act like Christ toward one's fellow Christians.

7. SC (DBWE1), 179–80.

Creating Community with the Seminarians of Finkenwalde

The opportunity to organize, with church backing, the kind of community Bonhoeffer had in mind came in 1935 when he accepted the directorship of the Confessing Church seminary in Pomerania. He had been approached in the summer of 1934 with the offer to be part of the Confessing Church's training of its future ministers. At the time Bonhoeffer had been contemplating a trip to India to study Gandhi's tactics of nonviolent resistance to systemic evil with a view to adopting Gandhi's practice against the repressive government of Adolf Hitler and Nazi fascism. He acquired letters of reference from Bishop George Bell of Chichester, and Reinhold Niebuhr, his former teacher at Union Seminary, and was formally accepted into Gandhi's ashram. But the trip to India never materialized. Instead, he agreed to direct the illegal seminary and help train future ministers as subversives within Hitler's Germany.

In preparation for this task he used his final months as pastor of two German-speaking parishes in London to visit Anglican monasteries and seminaries to examine their "monastic styled" training programs and their different modes of community life. Encouraged by his early theological and spiritual interests, Bonhoeffer resolved to establish the kind of training center for Germany's future moral leaders where everyone would be fully committed to incorporating Jesus' Sermon on the Mount into their daily life. This commitment would in turn be sustained by community structures based on the gospel, structures that emphasized their togetherness as well as their need for prayerful time alone and with others in order to foster the mutual support they needed and their service of one another as a prelude for serving the wider church-community. He wanted also to have incorporated into their lives a daily routine with regular spiritual exercises and hours of worship, manual work or housekeeping, classes on Christian discipleship, and ecumenical dialogue, all to reinforce their resistance to the systemic evil that had been the original motivation for establishing these Confessing Church seminaries. These seminaries were established in opposition to the Reich Church's seminaries then in the majority and highly supportive of Hitler and the Nazi ideology. Bonhoeffer made his intentions clear in a memorandum to the Ecumenical Youth Commission in 1935. There he stated that even before his appointment he and some compatible students had desired to start "a small Christian community in the form of a settlement or any other form on the basis of the Sermon on the Mount" and where "only by a clear and uncompromising stand [could] Christianity be a vital force for our people".[8]

However, the community life Bonhoeffer set in motion at Finkenwalde soon put him in violation of the laws of the Nazi government relating to the regulations for church affairs. He kept the seminarians focused, not on their dissident status, but on the purpose for their training. We read in *Life Together* his detailed account of how the day was to be spent in a structured balance of devotions, study, classes in discipleship and preaching, service of one another, common meals, and hours of worship, leisure, and play. What is not so clear in *Life Together* are the tensions Bonhoeffer had to endure in directing the seminary his way and in setting up a "Brothers house" to provide continuity to what was in practice an ex-

8. DB, 413.

periment in community living. He lectured extensively on what being disciples of Jesus Christ entailed for Christians eager to practice their faith in obedience to the gospel. Those lectures later became his spiritual classic, *Discipleship*. For the seminarians, the following of Jesus Christ in Bonhoeffer's way meant beginning each day with prayer and private meditation, for which they had little or no preparation. In those first meditation times, some read, some slept, some smoked, and some allowed their minds to wander. Some voiced their resentment at being the butt of jokes from ordinands at other seminaries about their "unevangelical monasticism."

All this was brought out in an evening discussion they had with Bonhoeffer on his return from a protracted absence from the seminary. He listened with sympathy to their complaints, but did not waver about their continuing to practice the daily meditation. Instead, he suggested that they have a communal meditation once a week. The public sharing of their meditation, in which Bonhoeffer himself took the lead, proved so helpful that gradually their opposition ceased. Most of them continued the practice after their seminary training. The daily meditation brought home to them that their faith had to be centered in God's word as a gift given to them in their relationship with God and not as a personal skill acquired for the sole purpose of impressing their parishioners in preaching.[9]

With the intention of helping them in their practice of meditation, Bonhoeffer introduced his seminarians to the *Losungen*, or short daily texts drawn from the Bible that the Moravians had been using and making available to a wide variety of interested people. In his circular letters both before and

9. CML, 153–55.

during the war, Bonhoeffer called his seminarians' attention to those texts, especially those that were appropriate for the time and the circumstances of their ministry. In Tegel Prison he declared that these daily texts had opened for him a whole new world of meaning. Before his imprisonment he included the weekly texts in his letters to the seminarians, reminding them of the "precious gift which is given us in meditation . . . which brings inward and outward order into my life [and] gives our life something like constancy. . . . It keeps us in the saving grace of our congregation, of our brothers and sisters, of our spiritual home."[10] For Bonhoeffer, these were the advantages of meditation in one's church-community life.

Bonhoeffer's Vision of Community Life

Bonhoeffer had argued that Chistian life could never be lived in the drab abstraction experienced in the typical German parishes of the day. The people needed a genuine Christian community. He was certain that the authentic profession of one's faith required living in community and developing a sensitivity to one another. Further, he pointed out that clericalism and the pursuit of clerical perquisities distracted church leaders from their calling to serve, not themselves or their buildings, but the needy people entrusted to their care. He challenged the churches, therefore, to renounce their clerical privileges and make themselves more available for generous, self-sacrificing service to the most vulnerable of God's people. This giving of themselves to others through whole-hearted living in a Christian community would focus the ministers on the Christ-centeredness of their calling. Finally, Bonhoeffer made it clear that the community life he envisaged could pro-

10. TF, 457.

vide pastors with a spiritual refuge where they could renew and refresh themselves for further service in the church.

In some respects, Bonhoeffer's vision of the kind of Community life needed in the church can still serve as a gauge of whether a Christian community is on the right track in its ability to live according to the gospel mandates. Bonhoeffer wrote of his priorities: "There are two things the brothers have to learn during their short time in the seminary—first, how to lead a community life in daily and strict obedience to the will of Christ Jesus, in the practice of the humblest and the noblest service one Christian brother can perform for another. . . . Secondly, they have to learn to serve the truth alone in their study of the Bible and its interpretation in their sermons and teaching."[11]

It came as a major disappointment to Bonhoeffer when the Gestapo closed down the seminary. He had been warned by his brother that he was in danger from the authorities for what to them appeared to be a "subversive act." His attempts to continue the training of seminarians through clandestine meetings were fraught with obstacles. They were unable to form communities such as existed in Finkenwalde. In the difficult, lonely days of his imprisonment, however, Bonhoeffer would derive solace from the lingering memories of community life in the seminary with its nurturing prayers and warm expressions of brotherly love for and service to one another. Because the community life at the Finkenwalde seminary was structured by a disciplined life not common to the Protestant tradition in Germany and a daily schedule that resembled somewhat the regimen of Catholic and Anglican monasteries, Bonhoeffer had to fend off accusations that he was catholiciz-

11. CML, 157.

ing the seminary or introducing a hothouse atmosphere that was both esoteric and impractical. He was able to win over his critics and the seminarians themselves by the introduction of several counterbalancing aspects of their life together.

First and foremost, he enabled the seminarians to experience, many for the first time, the sustaining power of a life in common in a faith-filled, caring community. Second, the ordinands were given rigorous theological, spiritual training that helped them to distinguish between the task of theological reflection and the demands of their ministry of pastoral care. Third, their daily routine was punctuated by periods of recreation, music, sports, and other forms of lighthearted relaxation. Bonhoeffer's biographer reports that Bonhoeffer was adept at organizing these periods of physical, mental, and spiritual renewal. Finally, Bonhoeffer was able to convince the seminarians and the church authorities that the life together he had set in motion was not a withdrawal from the arena of combat against Nazism in the churches. On the contrary, he intended their life together to be a unique, more effective way of preparing the young ministers to enter that struggle as moral leaders, and in the process to revitalize their church.[12]

The Writing and Publishing of *Life Together*

Bonhoeffer's community at Finkenwalde lasted only a little more than two years before it was closed down by the Gestapo. Prior to the Gestapo action he had been reluctant to publicize the noteworthy common life and unforgettable experiences he and his seminarians had lived through. But in 1938 and at a moment when it seemed that Hitler was about

12. See "Editor's Introduction," LT (DBWE 5), 20.

to invade Czechoslovakia and march the German nation into another war, Eberhard Bethge, Bonhoeffer's best friend, biographer and one of the brothers who had experienced the "life together" in that seminary, urged him to record for posterity what had taken place at Finkenwalde. Bonhoeffer finally agreed but with the intention to share with the German public his conviction that the wider church needed to develop a similar mode of Christian community if it wanted to be liberated from or immune to the seduction of ideologies like that of Adolf Hitler and Nazism. With a new sense of urgency triggered by the Sudetenland crisis, he and Bethge went in late 1938 to the home of his twin sister Sabine Leibholz in Göttingen to actually work on the text of *Life Together.* Earlier in the month the two of them had helped the Leibholz family to escape Germany into Basel, Switzerland, from which they later emigrated to the safe haven of Oxford, England, and the protection of Bishop George Bell.

Bonhoeffer completed work on *Life Together* in a single, hurried stretch of four weeks. The book itself was published in 1939. It is a testament to its popularity that within a year it had reached a fourth printing. Since then this spiritual classic has been through twenty-four reprints, in addition to the new critical edition and thoroughly revised translation for the Dietrich Bonhoeffer Works English Edition series and on which this entire section is based. The book's initial publication in German as *Gemeinsames Leben* (*Life Together*) was by Christian Kaiser Verlag as part of its series, *Theologische Existenz heute* (Theological Existence Today). It was revised in a fourth printing by the publishing house of Albert Lempp. The twentieth reprint in 1979 added a valuable "Afterword" by Eberhard Bethge that helped readers understand its original setting and impact. Following its twenty-first reprint in 1986, Kaiser Verlag published the new, critical edition in 1987 as volume 5 of the Dietrich Bonhoeffer Werke, which comprises seventeen volumes of the collected writings of Bonhoeffer in their original German. The first English translation of *Life Together* was by John Doberstein and published in 1954 by Harper and Row, then headquartered in New York. Like the German edition, this translation had undergone twenty-three reprintings.

The Editorial Board decided that *Life Together* would be the first of the volumes in the DBWE and assigned me the task of editing the book with careful attention to including and enhancing the German editors' critical apparatus. My "Introduction" to the text describes the many difficult problems associated with translating Bonhoeffer's German into the most accurate English faithful to Bonhoeffer's original intent and the exact meaning of his German terms. Like *Discipleship*, *Life Together* is now in a revised paperback edition and taking its place among both scholars who study Bonhoeffer and Christians everywhere who are inspired by Bonhoeffer's writings and especially interested in the dynamics of Christian community as described in this spiritual classic.

Bonhoeffer's Preface

When Bonhoeffer wrote his account of his efforts at creating a Christian community that would sustain the spiritual life in himself and his fellow seminarians in the Finkenwalde seminary, he was not reminiscing about an agreeable, idyllic experience of a like-minded group of dedicated seminarians. He intended to share this experience with others, with its joys and trials, its mutual support and enduring friendships, that it might serve as a model for forming moral leaders and for constructing new forms in church-community life throughout Germany. He was aware of how the churches had compromised their integrity by acquiescing in so many of the immoral policies and legislative acts of the Nazi government. Later he would accuse the churches for their complicity in the widespread destruction of life in the war and in the concentration camps. At the same time he had only vivid memories of how he and his seminarians were able to form a supportive community for each other before the Gestapo closed down the seminary.

Bonhoeffer wrote in his Preface, therefore, of his hope that what they accomplished could become a possibility for the church as a whole. In fact, it was entirely possible, he said, for the creation of communities like these to become a bona fide "mission entrusted to the church."[13] In depicting that community in *Life Together*, Bonhoeffer also acknowledged the urgent need for the church to discover different ways to be the church. He thus emphasized the courageous following of Jesus Christ within a genuine community formed along the lines of the gospel, not the typical kind of church gatherings where strangers met and remained strangers, and whose dull blandness offered little resistance to the political ideology that had successfully gained the allegiance of most churchgoers. The book itself is divided into five interrelated sections: Community, the Day Together, the Day alone, Service, and a final section on Confession and the Lord's Supper. In Bonhoeffer's concept of community, one's personal strengths should be supported in and through the sharing of conviction that takes place in a genuine Christian community where the

13. LT (DBWE 5), 25.

teachings of Jesus Christ, not fascist ideology, should inspire believers.

1. COMMUNITY

This section begins and ends with a passage from the Psalms proclaiming how good and pleasant it is when brothers and sisters can live together in unity (Ps 133:1). Bonhoeffer explained that the "unity" of which the Psalmist speaks is made possible through Jesus Christ who is the source of the peace that should reign in community. He does not claim that community life is without its tensions. Bonhoeffer was aware of his own sense of frustration in the church struggle and of the ever present danger of the Nazi persecution of anyone that dared resist or denounce their policies. He quoted Luther in reminding his seminarians that their community life was set in the midst of their most vicious enemies. He tells anyone embracing Christian community faithful to Jesus Christ and the gospel to be resigned to the inevitable antagonisms generated by well-armed enemies who demand absolute allegiance to their own ideology under threat of imprisonment and death.

This having been said, Bonhoeffer emphasized the strength of a Christian community as an indomitable defense against those who would destroy both their church and their nation. In that context he speaks of "the incomparable joy and strength" given to people of faith through "the physical presence of other Christians."[14] To live in community with other Christians is, he points out, a privilege and a blessing that should prompt a daily prayer of gratitude to God. He

14. LT (DBWE 5) 29.

adds that those who, in coming together, want more than what Jesus Christ has promised do not really want community. The Christian community does not offer the extraordinary, rhapsodic experiences that people might desire. Nor should they confuse Christian community with their wishful thinking and their personal pious projections. According to Bonhoeffer, those who declare their willingness to form such a community are not called to create a utopian ideal or to enjoy a self-centered worldly happiness. He insists that the Christian community is fundamentally a divinely established spiritual reality in its very core, but with all the practical challenges that individual Christians living in community must share and face.

Life Together moves from these opening cautions to an analysis of the dangers that can erode community life. "Wishful thinking," for example is the phrase he uses for those who ruin community togetherness by projecting their own image of what they imagine the common life should be. They are often the dreamers who annoy others in their insistence on having things their way with little room for compromise. Their idealized image is puffed up with the pride and pretentiousness that can lead to disillusionment. Instead of permitting those "wishful dreamers" to dominate the common life that others have embraced, Bonhoeffer counters with a call to forego one's wishful projections in favor of courageously accepting the reality of what God has *actually* accomplished in Jesus Christ. Gratitude for what God has done, not embittered carping over the failure of others to cooperate in one's unreal vision, should mark the attitudes of those who agree to share their faith in the unique ways of Christian community. For Bonhoeffer, this must include gratitude for the supportive presence of others, forbearance and forgiveness, and compassion for the weaker members of the community. In essence, Bonhoeffer asks those who commit themselves in faith to form a community life in union with Jesus Christ to engage in heartfelt gratitude for everything small or great. He counseled the community members not to be constantly complaining. He warned too against gauging the worthiness of one's personal spirituality on the artificial standards of grandiose achievement. Only God, he says, knows the true depths of the community's growth into Christ and the true contributions of the members.

According to Bonhoeffer, the quality of the love that binds the members together can either empower the community members to live for each other or it can stifle community spirit and ultimately prove fatal to the survival of their common life. As a forewarning against this danger Bonhoeffer contrasted what he called "spiritual love" with what he wanted to expose and counteract for its lethal flaws: the self-centered, purely emotional, self-gratifying giving in to one's urges under the guise of genuine love. Self-centered love, he said, is calculating, manipulative, and domineering. Spiritual love, on the contrary is humble, deferential, submissive to the guidance of God's Holy Spirit and God's word. This spiritual love is agapeic, capable of loving the other without preset conditions for the sake of Jesus Christ. Self-serving love, he argued, is incapable of loving one's enemies. Those addicted to it long for other persons in an emotionality that uses the others for their own purposes and often as objects of "uncontrolled and uncontrollable dark desires."[15] It can lead

15. LT (DBWE 5), 44.

to lustful enslavement and psychic domination for the sake of the pleasure one can derive from another.

Bonhoeffer was convinced that this kind of false love can lead to the exclusion from the community of the handicapped, the weak, and those labeled as insignificant and non-productive. Ultimately, self-centered love can cause the exclusion of Jesus Christ who, in the person of those rejected as less than desirable, begs the believer's compassion. Bonhoeffer reminds those who would form themselves into a Christ-centered community that they "must release others from all attempts to control, coerce, and dominate them with [their] love. In their freedom from [them], other persons want to be loved for who they are as those for whom Christ also became a human being, died and rose again, as those for whom Christ won the forgiveness of sins and prepared eternal life."[16]

In their spiritual love, on the other hand, Bonhoeffer urges Christians to recognize the true image of the other person from the perspective of Jesus Christ in whose image God has formed followers of Christ and whose image God wants to form in all peoples.

Bonhoeffer notes in concluding this section that the euphoric thrill of experiencing the love that genuine community makes possible is an unpredictable extra and not the sole purpose of community life. Faith, not fleeting emotional satisfaction, is what holds the Christian community together, engendering the more lasting joy and happiness that comes through living in communion with Jesus Christ and, in Jesus Christ, with one another.

16. LT (DBWE 5), 44.

2. THE DAY TOGETHER

Bonhoeffer was all too aware of the importance of structure for a community of Christians with a common faith. To that end, his practical side came through in the careful daily schedule of the time together for him and his seminarians. From rising in the morning until the public evening prayer there were always things to do. He offered practical directions in order to encourage their mutual support and to insure continuity in their community life. He insisted, therefore, on an early hour for communal worship, with time given to the singing of hymns, the reading of scripture, and prayer. That morning hour, he wrote, "does not belong to the individual; it belongs to all the church of the triune God, to the community of Christians living together, to the community of brothers."[17] His community began their life together each morning by gathering for worship with their prayers of praise and thanks, their scriptural readings, and their hymns breaking the silence of the nightly darkness.

Bonhoeffer insisted that his community consider their morning time sacred. He admitted frankly that he did not want them to "be burdened and haunted by the various kinds of concerns they face during that working day."[18] He taught them that in those early moments of prayer they had an opportunity to experience anew the mediation of Jesus Christ and the enlightenment of his word. He followed this exhortation with a lengthy explanation of the beauty and power of the Psalter. He declared that in the Psalms the community is drawn into the prayer of none other than Jesus Christ who, as vicarious representative of all Christians, stood with the

17. LT (DBWE 5), 49

18. LT (DBWE 5), 51.

individual and the community praying on behalf of all their needs.[19]

To this prayer Bonhoeffer conjoined the common reading of the scriptures. He believed such reading would have the effect of drawing the community into the stories of Israel and of Jesus, and in this way help the members of the community to learn more about their own stories. In effect, Bonhoeffer asked the Christian community to know the scriptures the way the great reformers did. For them, the Bible was a privileged gift from God for the spiritual nurturing of the people. Bonhoeffer conceded that too often the scriptures were excluded when one's practical course of action was to be determined. The subtle reference to the manner in which ordinary Germans and many of their churches hailed Hitler and the Nazi ideology without any reference to the biblical judgment or the teachings of Jesus Christ is unmistakable here. For Bonhoeffer, even when the biblical word goes against the grain of one's own selfish inclinations or one's political affiliation, it is not thereby to be discredited in favor of what the popular mood might dictate. What is more, Bonhoeffer questioned whether Christians, especially the leaders of Christian communities, can be of help to one another except through discernment of God's own word. He notes that mere human words fail to alleviate one's troubles and temptations.

Bonhoeffer found the singing of hymns in unison a pleasant spiritual exercise in which one's voice is united to others as the voice of the church itself. The words, together with the music, extend the spiritual horizons of the commu-

19. On Bonhoeffer's exhortation to the community to pray the Psalms daily and to appreciate the place of the Psalms in one's community life, see LT (DBWE 5), 58.

nity just as this mode of music making enhances the word of God and brings a unique dimension to community praise, thanksgiving, confession, and prayer. Feeble though the quality of the music or the quality of the individual voice may be—and here Bonhoeffer poked fun at the show-off "basso profundos" and quivering tenors who liked to dominate the music, and the moody members who, in their hurt feelings, refused to sing. For him, a musician himself, the singing of hymns helped the community joyfully and with the proper melody to become one with the song of the church.[20]

At the closing of the service Bonhoeffer strongly recommended that the members of the community bring up their requests, their expressions of gratitude, and intercessions in a common prayer.[21] He believed this practice had the power to break down one's fears of the reactions of others and the inhibitions one feels against praying freely and publicly in the presence of others. For Bonhoeffer, this common intercessory prayer in the name of Jesus Christ was "the most normal thing in our common Christian life."[22] Bonhoeffer would cap the common worship service with extemporaneous prayer led by an individual in the community, often the head of the house or director of the group. He adds the cautionary word, however, that the individuals who close the daily worship with a spontaneous prayer must be aware that they pray for the community as a whole and not in place of that community. Hence they have to share in the common life and know firsthand the community's needs and concerns, its joys and requests, its gratefulness for favors received and its hopes.

20. LT (DBWE 5), 65–66.

21. LT (DBWE 5), 68–69.

22. LT (DBWE), 69.

Nor must they confuse the possible chaos of their own heart with the more ordered hearts of others who also compose the community. He advises too against the temptation to substitute the profound, well-crafted, prefabricated prayers of the universal church for the more personal, though perhaps fumbling, confused prayer one must offer to God every day. On this point he argues that "here the poorest stammering can be better than the best phrased prayer."[23] He shared with the seminarians his impression that God is more moved by sincerity of heart than by impressive words that one strives to make as eloquent as possible.

Finally, Bonhoeffer turned his attention to the breaking of bread together, the meals, the Lord's Supper, and the heavenly banquet. The first of these is his main concern in their day together, namely, the role of the table fellowship in binding Christians to one another both spiritually and physically. The fostering of community at the hours of table repast serves to remind Christians of the providential care God takes of God's children and of the ways in which God has blessed God's people with the good gifts of food and drink. Bonhoeffer states clearly that he does not want to see these gifts spiritualized through misplaced begrudging of the body's need for comfort. Nor does he countenance eating in a somber, sullen, or non-celebratory fashion. The call to table fellowship, he says, is an invitation to be festive even in the midst of or at the end of one's working hours. In their enjoyment of these "good gifts," "Christians recognize their Lord as the true giver of all good gifts. And beyond this, they recognize their Lord as the true gift, the true bread of life itself, and as the one who calls them to the joyful banquet in the reign

23. LT (DBWE 5), 71.

of God."[24] They thus become, in a special way, bound to their Lord and to one another.

Bonhoeffer concluded his recommendations for the community's day together with the structure of evening prayer, a brief daily worship service with song. This is for him the moment when Christians can lay aside their work and entrust their cares to God. Most important of all, it seemed to him, was his plea that at the close of their day the members of the Christian community ask forgiveness of their sins against God and one another and express their forgiveness of any wrongs done to them. He counseled this practice vehemently, perhaps conscious of the vindictiveness then encouraged in government circles and accepted in resigned silence by the churches. "It is perilous," he wrote, "for the Christian to go to bed with an unreconciled heart. Therefore, it is a good idea especially to include the request for mutual forgiveness in every evening's prayers, so that reconciliation can be achieved and renewal of the community established."[25] Bonhoeffer set the day together to end the way it began, with prayers to the God who in Jesus Christ had made the Christian community possible—and necessary, for churches, nations, and individuals in turmoil—if one is to remain united in spirit with Jesus Christ.

3. The Day Alone

To claim, as Bonhoeffer did, that living together with others in community is actually strengthened by individual time alone strikes many readers as a paradox. For Bonhoeffer,

24. LT (DBWE 5), 73.
25. LT (DBWE 5), 79.

however, solitude in community is neither paradoxical nor a contradiction. He goes so far as to declare that "whoever cannot be alone should beware of community."[26] He is clear on the point that community was not an escape route for those unable to cope with life on their own, or for those who desire to bury bad experiences of their past with help from the companionship of gracious people. "The Christian community," he says, "is not a spiritual sanatorium" where one's sense of isolation can be healed.[27]

But Bonhoeffer also insisted that if people cannot endure living in community, they should also be wary of being alone. The Christian calling, he said, is to enter into a community of faith; it is not a call to isolated exercise of one's faith or a call suitable for the rugged individual who craves to be left alone at all times. Christians, genuine in their profession of allegiance to Jesus Christ, pray, act, and struggle with difficulties always in the sustaining communion with Jesus Christ and with other Christians. Bonhoeffer recognized, therefore, "that only as we stand within the community can we be alone, and only those who are alone can live in the community. Both belong together."[28]

What did Bonhoeffer intend by correlating the time set aside for being alone with the times spent with others in the personal exchanges that are part of every thriving community? He expanded the concept of "being alone" with the adjunct ideas of beneficial solitude and silence. In his opinion, both the individual believer and the community need the solitude and silence out of which comes the deepening

26. LT (DBWE 5), 83.
27. LT (DBWE 5), 82.
28. LT (DBWE 5), 83.

of one's appreciation for true community living. Bonhoeffer's affirmation of the need for solitude is similar to John Shelby Spong's observation that, "the most lonely, frustrated people I have worked with have not been the loners but people who are addicted to social interaction. Afraid to encounter themselves in solitude, they fill their lives with shallow social interactions that keep them from ever coming face to face with their own solitary spirit."[29]

The silence of which Bonhoeffer speaks is required to listen prayerfully to the word of God and to the words of those who share life in community. This is the silence needed to let God have the first word in the early morning hour and the last word as one ends the day in sleep. It helps the members of the community to avoid idle chatter and misuse of speech that can wound the most vulnerable members of the community; it helps people to manage their speech during their daily conversations. There is power, Bonhoeffer says, in this kind of silence, "the power of clarification, purification, and focus on what is essential" that contributes "to proper speaking of God's Word at the right time."[30]

For Bonhoeffer, the silence structured into their daily schedule is vital to that encounter with God's word that shapes the community. To protect this silence, Bonhoeffer advocated regular times for being alone: meditation on God's word in the scriptures, hours of prayer, and moments of intercession, all converging in the daily period of quiet meditation. This meditation, he insisted, serves the purpose of bringing order into one's daily life as it provides the "solid ground on which

29. CML, 166.
30. LT (DBWE 5), 85.

to stand and clear guidance for the steps we have to take."[31] This is the time for God's word to enter into human hearts to remain as an empowering, guiding force for the entire day. Bonhoeffer eschews any expectation of extraordinary, blissful experiences that might or might not occur in the period of silent meditation. On the other hand, neither spiritual aridity nor occasional listlessness should dissuade Christians from persevering in their meditative attention to the word of God spoken in silence.

Bonhoeffer depicts one's effective prayer life itself as an offshoot of this meditative listening to God's word. "Prayer," he claims, "means nothing else but the readiness to appropriate the Word, and what is more, to let it speak to me in my personal situation, in my particular tasks, decisions, sins and temptations."[32] This personal prayer thus complements what one may feel as an individual need but, for various reasons, can never enter it into the community prayer; instead, one makes these personal problems known to God alone in silent prayer.

Equally important for Bonhoeffer is intercessory prayer for one another. He sees intercession as a natural outcome of the agapeic love, whereby "Christians [bring] one another into the presence of God, seeing each other under the cross of Jesus as poor human beings and sinners in need of grace."[33] When this intercessory attitude can be fostered, the antagonisms that can tear a community apart are tempered. In the midst of the Nazi world where hurting the enemy was held up as deserving of medals of honor, Bonhoeffer offered the following extraordinary reason for intercessory prayer:

31. LT (DBWE 5), 87.
32. LT (DBWE 5), 89.
33. LT (DBWE 5), 90.

> A Christian community either lives by the intercessory prayers of its members for one another, or the community will be destroyed. I can no longer condemn or hate other Christians for whom I pray, no matter how much trouble they cause me. In intercessory prayer the face that may have been strange and intolerable to me is transformed into the face of one for whom Christ died, the face of a pardoned sinner. That is a blessed discovery for the Christian who is beginning to offer intercessory prayer for others.[34]

For Bonhoeffer, forbearance and forgiveness, two of the most important dynamics of Christian community life, intersect at the point of intercessory prayer. In Nazi Germany such intercessory prayer for one's enemies, as mandated by Jesus Christ, seemed to be the only wedge in an otherwise militarized violence aimed at hurting and destroying those enemies.

4. SERVICE

Bonhoeffer looked on the diversity of those who belong to Christian communities as another aspect of God's blessings and another way in which the spirit of Christ is enfleshed anew in the loving presence of Christians one to another. "People," he wrote, "are talented and untalented, simple and difficult, devout and less devout, sociable and loners. Does not the untalented person have a position to assume just as well as the talented person, the difficult person just as well as the simple one?"[35] Bonhoeffer knew firsthand the dynamics

34. LT (DBWE 5), 90.
35. LT (DBWE 5), 93.

of community living from his experiences at Finkenwalde. People come together in faith, but soon enough there follow the observations about those who share the common life, judgments of their character, and classifications of people according to standards that can plunge the community into a struggle for the soul of that community. Bonhoeffer warns the community against the competitiveness, domineering tendencies, exploitation of the weak, untalented, and invidious comparisons that are abhorrent to the spirit of Jesus Christ.

Instead, he counsels the community to look on their diversity, not as an enemy of the common life, but as a cause for rejoicing and an opportunity to strengthen the community bonds. Bonhoeffer implies that the community's strength lies in the care it takes of its weakest members. Hence the wisdom of his observation about the interaction of the weak and the strong. "Every Christian community must know that not only do the weak need the strong, but also that the strong cannot exist without the weak. The elimination of the weak is the death of the community."[36] These are words written in the face of the Nazi determination to euthanize the mentally and emotionally weak and physically handicapped.

The core of Bonhoeffer's concerns is to integrate diversity into the formation of a community faithful to Jesus Christ in the promotion of mutual service that, like common worship, scripture reading, table fellowship, and holding to the daily schedule, is necessary for the community to grow in love for one another and into the image of Jesus Christ. He listed three kinds of services that one Christian must offer to

36. LT (DBWE 5), 96.

another for the sake of Jesus Christ and to keep the ideal of agapeic love alive within the community.

The first service mentioned in Bonhoeffer's encouraging the community to serve one another is that of *listening* to others. This, he says, is the work of God who is the great listener. Bonhoeffer was aware that preachers often overwhelmed their people with words when the people craved nothing more than the sympathetic ear of someone willing to listen to their problems. If we can't listen to one another, he asked rhetorically, how can we listen to God? "The death of the spiritual life starts here, and in the end there is nothing left but empty spiritual chatter and clerical condescension which chokes on pious words."[37] Bonhoeffer was insistent that if a person's time is too important to allow listening with patience to others, then that person really had no time for God.

The second great service for Bonhoeffer is *active helpfulness*. He is not advocating here those grandiose deeds that are often used to measure human greatness, but the simple help in the little things that can become bothersome in a community. Here Bonhoeffer focuses on an attitude fairly common in a structured life where some people may be engaged in important tasks and who appear not to tolerate any interruption. Often Christians may think their time or their plans too vital to what they hope to accomplish in any given day and so they may resent the knock of a needy brother or sister on the door or the intrusion into their plans for the next couple of hours. Bonhoeffer's counsel is that Christians must look on those unforeseen moments as opportunities to respond to none other than God who sends those needy people to busy Christians, however preoccupied they might be. "Nobody is

37. LT (DBWE 5), 98.

too good for the lowest service," he writes. "Those who worry about the loss of time entailed by such small, external acts of helpfulness are usually taking their own work too seriously. We must be ready to allow ourselves to be interrupted by God, who will thwart our plans and frustrate our ways time and again, even daily, by sending people across our path with their demands and requests."[38] Bonhoeffer concludes that, if we fail to make ourselves available for these small acts of service, we may be passing by the cross that God has raised across our lives to tell us that God's ways, not our own ways, are what count in the Christian community.

In a final segment, Bonhoeffer speaks of the *service of forbearance*. Drawing from Paul's advice to the Christians of Galatia, "bear with one another's burdens, and in this way you will fulfill the law of Christ" (Gal 6:2), he explains that Paul's words would never be a problem to pagans because pagans could simply stay away from burdensome people. Not so with Christians living in community! Bonhoeffer proposes as their example, not a proponent of secular wisdom on how to deal with others, but Jesus Christ himself, in whom God suffered by bearing with the flaws of his followers and enduring the sinfulness of his fellow human beings, even to the extent of making common cause with those regarded as disreputable and sinful. Bearing with human sin and forgiving sinners, he says, was the mission of Jesus Christ. Can it be otherwise for Christians?[39] For Bonhoeffer this forbearance is also how God draws Christians into a saving community in and with God's son Jesus. Only in this way can the freedom of others, including difficult sinners, be made possible. The implica-

38. LT (DBWE 5), 99.

39. LT (DBWE 5), 100–102.

tions of this attitude are enormous. In Christian forbearance the strong help the weak, the healthy help those who are ill, the talented help the untalented, the righteous help the fallen away sinner—always in a Christlike manner that is humble, patient, gentle, and friendly. According to Bonhoeffer, even the sinners must be forgiven on a daily basis.[40]

Bonhoeffer concludes this section of *Life Together* with the observation that listening, helping those in need, or bearing with others are ultimately the services that Christians are called to give by the word of God. That word, in turn, must be uttered freely to one another. To be the instrument of God's accepting, forgiving, peace-giving word is to give comfort as well as to offer forgiveness, admonition, and consolation. The service of forgiveness and forbearance was intended by Bonhoeffer as a practical way of providing an occasion for God to speak words of concern for, as well as, when annoyed, forbearance toward one's brothers or sisters, and to offer personal strength through the love of one Christian for another. For him, this was a Christlike way of being with and for one another even when hurt feelings could erupt. The call to service was an integral way for Bonhoeffer to help the community discern the importance of deepening their personal and spiritual relationships, which were so integral to their common life. In this Christlike way of being with and for one another Bonhoeffer discerns the deepening of personal and spiritual relationships that are integral to the common life that takes place in Christian communities.

40. LT (DBWE 5), 105–6.

5. Confession and the Lord's Supper

In the last segment of *Life together*, Bonhoeffer emphasizes the need for Christians to confess their sins to a representative of the Christian community. He states unequivocally his belief that the call to confession is essential for those living together, that they might confront their sins directly, particularly the sins and failings that have had an impact on the community's well-being. Despite the fact that the practice of confession of sins had fallen into disuse in Protestant Germany, Bonhoeffer took seriously the scriptural injunction to "confess your sins to one another" (James 5:16). He also invokes John 20:23 in directing the members of the Christian community to admit their sins in confession to another member of the community.

On the practical level, Bonhoeffer looks on this confession as an opportunity for Christians to drop their masks, their pretenses, and their denials, and to acknowledge what they are in God's sight: sinners who have experienced God's mercy. "In Christ," he writes, "the love of God came to the sinner. In the presence of Christ human beings were allowed to be sinners, and only in this way could they be helped. Every pretense came to an end in Christ's presence. This was the truth of the gospel in Jesus Christ: the misery of the sinner and the mercy of God. The community of faith in Christ was to live in this truth."[41] Bonhoeffer notes further that in the act of confessing one's sins, other Christians have the occasion to become Christ for us. They are now the sign of God's gracious, caring, forgiving presence. They are, in effect, sent by God to help us. The other Christian to whom we go to confess

41. LT (DBWE 5), 109.

sins hears us "in Christ's place, forgives our sins in Christ's name. Another Christian keeps the secret of our confession as God keeps it."[42]

Bonhoeffer hails the confession of sins as achieving a fourfold blessing: a breakthrough to community, a breakthrough to the cross, a breakthrough to new life, and a breakthrough to assurance of being in the graced presence of Jesus Christ. Relieved of the burden of sin, the Christian now stands relieved in the community of sinners, living by the forgiving grace of God in the cross of Jesus Christ. Sin exposed and forgiven loses its power. Bonhoeffer sees confession as providing a necessary opportunity for sinners to break with their past. The renunciation of sin shatters sin's power, delivers the Christian believer from the darkness of evil and brings with it the conversion and the longed-for new life in which one's baptism is renewed and the following of Jesus Christ reaffirmed.[43]

In the direction of his community that he describes in *Life Together*, Bonhoeffer was trying to reinforce a consciousness of personal sins as well as of the sins that threatened community. This was one of the reasons why he linked the confession of sins to preparation for the celebration of the Lord's Supper, the sacrament that celebrated their common life and their communion with both Jesus Christ and one another. The reconciliation that was the outcome of having their sins forgiven was, in his opinion, the best preparation for those who desired to receive the body and blood of Jesus Christ and, in that communion, to renew their commitment to one another, symbolized in the Lord's Supper. One must

42. LT (DBWE 5), 109.

43. See LT (DBWE 5), 111–14.

not approach the table of the Lord unprepared. Hence all anger, envy, contention, hurtful gossip—in a word, any sin detrimental to those who composed the community—had to be eliminated. The Lord's Supper, he notes, "is a joyous occasion for the Christian community. Reconciled in their hearts with God and one another, the community of faith receives the gift of Jesus Christ's body and blood, therein receiving forgiveness, new life, and salvation."[44] Bonhoeffer's closing words are a fitting summary of the kind of Christian community that is at once faithful in practice to the teachings of Jesus Christ and the source of that joy that Christians are called to find and enhance in one another. "Here joy in Christ and Christ's community is complete. The life together of Christians under the Word of God has reached its fulfillment in the sacrament."[45]

Questions

1. Does Bonhoeffer's criticism of the church in 1932 and later from prison apply to the church today?
2. How does one put into practice Bonhoeffer's statement that Christians are called to be Christ for others? What do you make of his statement that "whoever lives in love is Christ in relation to the neighbor?
3. How might Bonhoeffer's community structures in his *Life Together* help to restructure today's churches?
4. What are the advantages of solitude, private prayer, and meditation for one's personal contribution to the common life in community?

44. LT (DBWE 5), 118.
45. LT (DBWE 5), 118.

5. How do the three forms of service advocated by Bonhoeffer, listening to one another, active helpfulness even in little things, and forbearance/forgiveness converge within one's life together in the church-community?
6. Why does Bonhoeffer believe that the confession of sins and the Lord's Supper are essential to sustaining the mutual love expressed in one's communion with Christ and one another in the Christian community? How can these practices enhance parish life today?

FOUR

Selected Writings on Peace: An Ecumenical Conference and Two Sermons

Introduction

Students discovering Dietrich Bonhoeffer for the first time are fascinated by the fact that this moral leader who involved himself in a plot to kill Adolf Hitler was not only an ordained minister, but also throughout a large portion of his professional career a spokesperson for activism on behalf of peace and for maintaining a peace ethic in an era of Nazi militarism and Hitler's instigating a world war. In this section of the book we will examine three texts in which Bonhoeffer reveals himself as an uncompromising advocate for peace on the troubled earth where Nazism ruled with tactics of fear, violence, and the promise of a return to German military glory. Even when, as the circumstances of mass killings on the battlefields and in the concentration camps dictated, Bonhoeffer abandoned his espousal of nonviolence to join the conspiracy, a peace ethic not only remained his ideal but also a central core of his moral teachings. Before the conspiracy entered its critical phase, there were identifiable moments when Bonhoeffer publicly taught that the only way to do God's will in following Jesus Christ was to live out Jesus' teachings on non-violent resistance to societal and governmental injustices.

While it is difficult to pinpoint the precise time when Bonhoeffer began to see war and pacifist activism in an entirely new light, there is clear evidence that the most significant shift in his attitude came in 1930–31 as a result of his close friendship with the French pacifist Jean Lasserre. Lasserre prompted his German friend to reread and reexamine the challenges of the Sermon on the Mount. He and Bonhoeffer engaged in long discussions over how war and the gospel were clearly contradictory. Gradually, Bonhoeffer came to understand more personally the absurdity of Christians killing people for the sake of national pride, economic advantages, hatred, revenge, territorial expansion, or some trumped up form of national security—the most common reasons for nations' declaring war on one another.

In private interviews, some in published form, Lasserre has said that he was drawn to Bonhoeffer because they were both international students on Sloan Fellowships at Union Theological Seminary and also because they represented the more serious European approach to theology. Lasserre suspected that his convictions on social Christianity and pacifism may have shocked Bonhoeffer at first because Bonhoeffer was, like most Germans, resentful of the harsh conditions imposed on Germany by the Treaty of Versailles following the Great War. In an interview just before his death, Lasserre described an important aspect of his initial attraction to Bonhoeffer: "He never crushed us with his theological superiority. He never let us feel that he disapproved of something in us or our behavior. He totally respected our freedom, that of living as well as thinking."[1]

Lasserre believed the turning point in Bonhoeffer's own pacifism came on a Saturday afternoon when together they viewed the film, "All Quiet on the Western Front," an openly anti-war movie. They were aghast and saddened to the point of tears at the lighthearted reaction of the young children in the theater to the killing portrayed on screen. They seemed to enjoy and even cheer the violence. Lasserre said that this was a shocking, even tragic experience for both of them. "I think it was there both of us discovered that the communion, the community of the church is much more important than the national community." Lasserre adds in his recollection of the event: "I think this has been very important in his path toward pacifism because he has discovered that war is not the most important thing from the church's viewpoint. The important, the only really important thing, is that the church . . . keep in fellowship with all Christians. And what is absolutely awful and unacceptable in war is that *Christians are compelled to forget their Christian faith*."[2]

Bonhoeffer's efforts to bring about world peace and the reconciliation of peoples in a Germany apparently preparing for another war were at once his deepest passion and his greatest frustration. His evolving views on peace, non-violence, forgiveness of enemies, and forbearance expressed in the ecumenical conference and sermons included here mark him as a strong advocate of a peace ethic in a nation where

1. Nelson, "Relationship of Jean Lasserre to Dietrich Bonhoeffer's Peace Concerns," 74.

2. Nelson, "Relationship of Jean Lasserre to Dietrich Bonhoeffer's Peace Concerns," 74; emphasis mine.

military glory was endlessly celebrated. In a recent article, Bonhoeffer scholar Clifford Green has argued convincingly that Bonhoeffer's Christian peace ethic lies at the very core of Bonhoeffer's theology and is integrated into his Christology, his lectures and book on discipleship, and very obviously in his *Ethics*. Green adds that even during his part in the coup d'état and in his writings on tyrranicide, Bonhoeffer never abandoned his peace ethic.[3] For Bonhoeffer, who eschewed reducing ethics to a priori general principles, fidelity to God's will, discerned in the exemplary life and teachings of Jesus Christ, would be the liberating force for Christians to embrace peace and reject war.

1. "THE CHURCH IS DEAD": A Lecture Presented at the International Youth Conference Of The Universal Christian Council on Life and Work and the World Alliance for Promoting International Friendship through the Churches, Gland, Switzerland, August 29, 1932

Background Context

Bonhoeffer's talk at this conference was originally to have been delivered by Bishop Valdemar Ammundsen, a Danish leader in the World Alliance. But when Ammundsen was unable to speak at the conference, the task fell to Bonhoeffer. His talk moved even the British to correct their initial view that he represented too pessimistic an attitude toward the world situation and toward the church's effectiveness in rectifying the problems the ecumenical council was addressing. Bonhoeffer himself, ever the pragmatist, had been apprehensive of the

3. See Green, "Pacifism and Tyrannicide."

British delegates' tendency to push toward statements and resolutions to buoy up people's spirits in effecting change as if the total task of the council lay more in its captivating statements rather than its practical deeds in favor of peace and justice. Bonhoeffer noted that the church's primary confession of faith, followed by practical actions and confrontations with the world's political powers, should be their focus. Here, as later, he advocatated for a "qualified silence" rather than official proposals and well-worded, pious resolutions they could boast of. He opened the conference, therefore, with the electrifying statement that the church was to all practical purposes a dead entity as far as the unbelieving world was concerned.

Bonhoeffer appeared, indeed, to be pessimistic in his examination of the church's call to help Europe and the world to "be conquered a second time by Christ." His opening words alluded to the church's continuing ineffectiveness in promoting peace and justice in a world that appeared to be gearing up for another conflict between nations. In his talk he dwellt on the delegates' common anxiety that "everything which we undertake here as church action could be too late, superfluous, even trivial."[4] But this gathering was also, he argued, the church in which there has been proclaimed "life to the dying." Because death and life come into contact in the cross of Christ, Christians and their churches cannot sink into a confusing pessimism or get overly buoyed up in a false optimism. Bonhoeffer states his conviction categorically, that "Christ is our peace. He alone exorcizes the idols and the demons [of war]. The world trembles only before the cross, not before us."[5] Because of the church's declared solidarity with Jesus

4. TF, 102.

5. TF, 104.

Christ. Bonhoeffer counsels the ecumenical delegates not to or get overly buoyed up in a misplaced optimism and not to sink into a confusing pessimism. They would, he concludes, cease to follow Christ if they ever approved of war; they would be equally unfaithful if they did nothing to prevent war. Bonhoeffer shares his view that the church was in danger of becoming entrapped by a naïve trust in the divided world, where violence between Nazis and Bolsheviks and their alluring promises were commonplace and a threat to the very life of the church. The church, he said, was near death because of its having compromised its integrity in making unholy alliances with the political world. In this talk we read too of his condemnation of the idolatry of national security, which was fueling the rise of fascism and which would lead to several destructive wars of the twentieth century. What the church should do to proclaim Christ in such a world is at the heart of the selection that follows, summed up in Bonhoeffer's passionate plea to "let Christ be Christ."[6]

In this excerpt, we see also Bonhoeffer's emphasis on the mystical body of Jesus Christ, who, as he insists, encounters Christians in one another. In Bonhoeffer's words: "Christ encounters us in our brother and sister, in the English, the French, the German."[7] These words will likewise be incorporated in a later sermon in which he denounces war in terms that equates the senseless killing of Christian by Christian as tantamount to killing Christ. The most dramatic section of the conference came with Bonhoeffer's litany of the world's troubles. The delegates of the World Alliance were meeting at a time when millions of people were suffering from hunger,

6. TF, 103.

7. TF, 103.

poverty, humiliation, hatred, and political extremism. And, in the midst of such degradation, it seemed that all the nations wanted to do was to dwell on their petty hatreds and arm themselves. This dangerous path Bonhoeffer denounced because it only added to the troubles between nations caught in the web of suspicion and mistrust, thinking they can protect their peace by additional weaponry. Their worship, Bonhoeffer notes, is not of Jesus Christ but the idolatry of national security.[8] The words he spoke at that ecumenical conference are strikingly relevant to today's world where nations continue to invoke national security as the prime reason for their obscene military expenditures at the expense of social programs for the needy who go begging. National security was destined to become the justification of the many wars since Bonhoeffer first spoke those words to the ecumenical alliance of churches that he believed could do something positive to live up to its divine mandate to promote peace on earth.

Here, too, we find Bonhoeffer condemning war as annihilating God's creation, obscuring God's revelation, and causing a stumbling block for the church, which, should it sanction war, would be guilty of disobedience to Jesus Christ and constitute a denial of his cross and what it stands for. By August 1932, Bonhoeffer's attraction to nonviolence and his rejection of war had grown close to the position of a more active pacifism. War was then seen by him as a grievous violation of the overarching Christian mandate to preserve life and follow Jesus even to the cross. The church, he declares, can only advocate for peace. Yet, at the same time, he cautions against accepting just any kind of peace. Bonhoeffer insists

8. TF, 104.

that peace must always be accompanied by justice and truth. He declares, therefore, that a peace without justice could be worse than the actual conflict in which systemic injustice may have played a part.[9] It seems that Bonhoeffer is alluding in those final words to the infamous peace treaty of Versailles whose unjust terms against Germany was used by Adolf Hitler as a prelude to and justification for the war he would later launch against Germany's "enemies."

In an earlier talk at the ecumenical conference in Czechoslovakia he had declared that war destroyed both body and soul to the extent that it could in no way be in accord with God's commandment. "War," he said, "needs idealizing and idolizing to be able to survive; war today, and therefore the next war, must be utterly rejected by the church. . . . Nor should we shy away from using the word pacifism today."[10] That sentence was a deliberate challenge to Germany's exaltation of the military hero and its inveterate contempt for pacifists. Bonhoeffer shared with these ecumenical leaders his fears that the ecumenical movement would be content with pleasant socializing but with no concrete move toward the most pressing issues that directly and indirectly affected the credibility of the church.

Excerpts from the Text of Bonhoeffer's Talk

> The unbelieving world says the church is dead; let us celebrate its funeral with speeches and confer-

9. TF, 104.

10. Bonhoeffer, "A Theological Basis for the World Alliance?" in *No Rusty Swords*, 170.

ences and resolutions, which all do it honor. The unbelieving world, full of pious illusions, says the church is not dead; it is only weak, and we will serve it with all our might and put it on its feet again. Only goodwill can do that; let us make a new morality.

The believer says: the church lives in the midst of death, only because God calls it from death to life, because God does the impossible toward us and through us—so would we all say. . . .

In all that we say and do we are concerned with nothing but Christ and his honor among people. Let no one think that we are concerned with our own cause, with a particular view of the world, a definite theology or even with the honor of the church. We are concerned with Christ and nothing else. Let Christ be Christ.

We come together to hear Christ. Have we heard him? I can only put the question all persons must answer for themselves. But I will say at least this: Is it not precisely the significance of these conferences that where someone approaches us appearing so utterly strange and incomprehensible in his or her concerns and yet demands a hearing of us, we perceive in the voice of our brother or sister the voice of Christ himself, and do not evade this voice, but take it quite seriously and listen and love these others precisely in their strangeness? We encounter each other in all openness and truthfulness and need, and we claim the attention of others. That is the sole way in which Christ encounters us at such a conference. We are here and we are joined together, not as the community of those who know, but of those who all look for the Word of their Lord and seek everywhere if they cannot hear it, not as those who know, but as those who seek, those who are hungry, those who wait, those who are in need, those who hope. Christ encounters us in our brother and sister, in the English, the French, the German. . . .

The World Alliance is the community of those who would hearken to the Lord as they cry fearfully to their lord in the world and in the night, and as they mean not to escape from the world, but to hear in it the call of Christ in faith and obedience, and as they know themselves responsible to the world through this call. It is not the organ of church action, grown weary of meditating upon the Word of God, but it is the church which knows of the sinfulness of the world and of Christianity, which expects all good things from God, and which would be obedient to this God in the world.

Why does the community of brothers and sisters as it is shown forth in the World Alliance exhibit fear in the church of Christ? Because it knows of the command for peace and yet, with the open eyes which are given to the church sees reality dominated by hatred, enmity, and power. It is as though all the powers of the world had conspired together against peace: money, business, the lust for power, indeed even love for the fatherland have been pressed into the service of hatred. Hatred of nations, hatred of people against their own countrymen. It is already flaring up here and there—what are the events in the Far East and in South America but a proof that all human ties are dissolving to nothing, that there is no fear of anything where the passion of hatred is nourished and breaks out? Events are coming to a head more terribly than ever before—*millions hungry*, people with cruelly deferred and unfulfilled wishes, desperate men who have nothing to lose but their lives and will lose nothing in losing them—humiliated and degraded nations who cannot get over their shame—*political extreme against political extreme, fanatic against fanatic*, idol against idol, and behind it all a world which bristles with weapons as never before, a world which feverishly arms itself to guarantee peace through weaponry, a world whose idol has become the word *security*—a world without sacrifice, full of mistrust and suspicion, because past fears are still with it—a humanity which trembles at itself, a humanity which is not sure of itself and is ready at any time to lay violent hands on itself—how can one close one's eyes at the fact that the demons themselves have taken over the rule of the world, that it is the powers of darkness who have here made an awful conspiracy and could break out at any moment? . . .

Christ must become present to us in preaching and in the sacraments just as in being the crucified one he has made peace with God and with humanity. The crucified Christ is our peace. He alone exorcizes the idols and the demons. The world trembles only before the cross, not before us.

And now the cross enters this world out of joint. Christ is not far from the world, not in a distant region, of our existence. He went into the lowest depths of our world, his cross is in the midst of the world. And this cross of Christ now calls wrath and judgment over the world of hatred and proclaims peace. Today there must be no more war—the cross

> will not have it. People must realize that nothing happens without strife in the world fallen from God, but there must be no war. War in its present form annihilates the creation of God and obscures the sight of revelation. War as a means of struggle can as little be justified from the necessity of struggle as torture as a legal means can be justified from the need for law. The church renounces obedience [to Christ] should it sanction war. The church of Christ stands against war for peace among people, between nations, classes, and races.
>
> But the church also knows that there is no peace unless righteousness and truth are preserved. A peace which does damage to righteousness and truth is no peace, and the church of Christ must protest against such peace. There can be a peace which is *worse than struggle*. But it must be a struggle out of love for the other, a struggle *of the spirit, and not of the flesh*.[11]

2. "The Cross of Christ and Remembrance of the Dead": Sermon Given on the Day of National Mourning, Berlin, February 21, 1932

Background Context

As was noted above, the influence on Bonhoeffer of the French pacifist, Jean Lasserre, founder of the "Movement for Reconciliation" in France, stirred him personally to rethink his ideas on war and helped him rediscover the words on peace and justice in Jesus Christ's Sermon on the Mount. His biog-

11. TF, 102–4.

rapher called this a "momentous change" in Bonhoeffer.[12] He had acknowledged to his brother, the physicist Karl-Friedrich, that the Sermon on the Mount had set him straight for the first time in his life. "I believe that inwardly I shall be really clear and honest only when I have begun to take seriously the Sermon on the Mount." He added the memorable words that reveal to what extent Jesus' words had captivated his heart. "At present there are still some things for which an uncompromising stand is worthwhile. And it seems to me that *peace and social justice or Christ himself are such*."[13] Peace and social justice soon became the main focus of Bonhoeffer's spiritual energies. Speaking before the German Student Christian Movement in Berlin in 1932, for instance, he linked following Christ with "becoming witnesses for peace." He jolted his youthful audience with his sharp, uncompromising insistence on uniting a professed faith in Christ with the bringing about of peace. In the talk he dismissed the phoniness of so many peace treaties in which considerations of national security dominated the more important issues of human dignity and the gospel demands. Among the more significant phrases, the following cuts to the heart of his argument: "So long as the world is without God, there will be wars. For Christ, rather, it is a matter of our loving God and standing in discipleship to Jesus in whom we are called with the promise of blessedness to become witnesses for peace." He rejected the political ethic that, in time of war, one is justified in stepping around the command of God that "you shall not kill," and the word of

12. DB, 203.

13. TF, 426; emphasis mine.

Jesus Christ to "love your enemies." That sort of unchristian casuistry, he says, only cheapens grace.[14]

The vehemence of Bonhoeffer's resistance to the glorification of war is seen further in his sermon on the "Day of National Mourning" (excerpted below)—the German equivalent, set in wintertime, of the American celebration of Memorial Day. Speaking to a congregation gathered to commemorate the war dead and with several of those in attendance wearing their military uniforms bedecked with medals of honor, Bonhoeffer spoke the daring words that in the name of Jesus Christ, Christians must reject war as one of the insidious powers attempting to wipe the spirit of Jesus Christ from Christian consciousness. Knowing that Nazism's promotion of war and that the military industrial powers were being used by Hitler in his promise to "liberate" Germany from the shame of losing the Great War and from the lingering effects of the depression, Bonhoeffer accused Germany's warmongers of attempting to replace the spirit of Jesus Christ with the language of political expediency. Knowing too that soldiers are thrilled by allusions to their being on the side of God as their leaders pep them up to kill the enemy and be willing to shed their own blood "for God and country," Bonhoeffer called those deceitful tactics a deliberately imposed confusion of fighting "in the name of Christ against the true Christ." In this sermon he wanted to expose the national and international deceit that in essence was aimed at seducing Christians away from following Christ's teachings on peace and justice. The "military industrial complex" under the cover of protecting the nation is, following Bonhoeffer's argument in this

14. TF, 94–95; see also CML, 103.

sermon, actually worshipping, not the Christian God, but the idol of national security, while tricking the citizens into believing that their expensive, though profitable, preparations for war were good for them and their nation.

At the outset of the Great War, George Bernard Shaw said something similar, namely, that the Bishops were rallying their flock around the altar of Mars. They may have been acting patriotically but they were, in effect, turning Jesus Christ into Mars. Agnostic and cynic though he was, he suggested that at the beginning of any war, the stock markets ought to be closed and the churches ought to be honest enough to close their doors until peace is declared.[15] One can only wonder how effective such a measure would be. For Bonhoeffer, however, in 1932 it was an uphill battle to turn the people of Germany against war. He was well aware of the argument that the politicians were the only ones speaking the language of reality, whereas Christ had nothing practical or relevant to offer when the issue was national security or defending one's nation from the enemy who might be aiming its weapons of mass destruction their way. This tactic Bonhoeffer did not hesitate to call a full rebellion against Jesus Christ and his teachings aided and abetted by the churches. His words rang with indignation as he exposed the fraud behind the political propagandizing of soldiers. Soldiers were being trained to purge their minds of Jesus Christ in order to do the murderous work of an army in battle. His critical exposure of these successful militaristic tactics could attest to the truth of Chesterton's complaint that Christianity had not failed; it had never even been tried.

15. Shaw, "Common Sense about the War," 60–61.

In 1936, on another day of national mourning, officially renamed by the Nazi government the "Day for Commemorating the Nation's Heroes," obviously referring only to soldiers fallen in the Great War, Bonhoeffer again preached against war. After offering the consolation of the gospel to those honoring their dead and expressing their grief at their loss, he led the congregation to ponder the meaning of wartime death. He mentioned that the change of name indicated also a change of attitude toward the war of 1914–1918. Sorrow had given way to pride in the achievements, sacrifice, and the heroic service of the soldiers for their country. Their sufferings for the people back home, he said, were embarrassing to those gathered to commemorate and mourn their loss. But, he asked, what did this mean for the people living in the mid 1930s who were still called to seek God above all? Bonhoeffer then pictured for his congregation a war photo showing the crucified Christ set in the middle of the barbed wire of a destroyed army trench. That symbol, he declared, is a graphic reminder that Christians, fully aware of the horrors of war, are called by Jesus Christ to repentance. Whether it be victory, struggle, or defeat, the question is whether Christians have really listened to the preaching of Christ, whether they have moved from their sorrow and pride in wartime to repentance. He then shared his reasons why he believed repentance was called for. "Our world is a forlorn world. . . . since war is a sin against God's gospel of peace. . . . Christendom and the churches had become largely responsible for the war by blessing it and declaring it justified before God." Repentance was called for "because Christians were fighting against Christians, because the world war was a war among Christian peoples against one another." Then alluding to the photo of Christ crucified, he added, "Christ in the trenches—that means a judgment against a godless world." He ended the sermon by proclaiming that in the face of war, Christians should indeed pray for their leaders, but also offer daily prayers for peace. "Christianity," he said, "pleads and prays only for peace."[16]

Excerpts from the Text of Bonhoeffer's Sermon

> Who would not be disturbed and ask: What is the meaning of the 1914–1918 event, what is the meaning of the millions of dead German men—for me—for us today? How does God speak through this? That means still one more time to ask quite simply: How can I put into one thought the idea of God, Christ, and the event of war? Should I say: it was an action of God, or should I give up hope and say: here God's might was at an end? Here Christ was far distant? . . . The wondrous theme of the Bible that frightens so many people is that the only visible sign of God in the world is the cross. Christ is not carried away from earth to heaven in glory, but he must go to the cross. And precisely there, where the cross stands, the resurrection is near; even there, where everyone begins to doubt God, where everyone despairs of God's power, there God is whole, there Christ is active and near. Where it is on a razor's edge, whether one becomes faithless or remains loyal—there God is, and there Christ is. Where the power of darkness does violence to the

16. *Illegale Theologen-Ausbildung: Finkenwalde 1935–1937* (DBW 14), 766–67. See the bibliography for the English language translation and critical edition of this volume now in progress under DBWE 14.

light of God, there God triumphs and judges the darkness. So is it also, when Christ thinks about the day that is approaching his congregation. His disciples ask him about the signs of his return after his death. This is not a return, happening but once. The end time in the Bible is the whole time and every day between the death of Christ and the last judgment. Yes, so seriously, so decisively does the New Testament see the death of Christ. . . .

Christ, however, knows that his way goes to the cross; that also the way for his disciples does not lead gloriously and safely directly into heaven, but that they too must go through the darkness, through the cross. Also, they must struggle. For that reason the first sign of the nearness of Christ—worthy enough of him!—is that their enemies become great, that the power of temptation, of apostasy, of unfaithfulness, becomes strong, that their congregation would be led right up to the abyss of confusion about God. The first will be that their enemies are concealed behind the name of Christ, and now under the appearance of Christ-likeness would entice us away from him. That is, the name "Christ" doesn't do it; and how easy it is in times of confusion as at present, to fight in the name of Christ against the true Christ. Then, however, when the spirits are once confused, the powers of the world are revealed, and burst forth openly. The powers that want to snatch the disciples from him, that want to show them that it is madness to go with him, that Christ has no power, only words; that they, the powers of reality, speak the language of facts and this language is more convincing than the language of Christ. The world bands together against the spirit of Christ, the demons are enraged: *it is a revolt against Christ. And the great power of the rebellion is called—war!* The others are called pestilence and expensive times. Thus, war, sickness, and hunger are the powers, who wish to take Christ's rule, and they are all incited by the archenemy of Christ, who is the living one from death. It would thus appear as though with Christ the victory is won. Christ has conquered Death, but now these powers are howling: we are here! Look at us and be terrified. We have might! Our power has not been taken from us. Christ has not won the victory, but we are winning the victory. Christ is dead. But we are living. We are called war, sickness, and hunger. Why do you let yourselves be bewitched by these false prophets who speak about peace and life, about God and the kingdom? We are here!

And they fall upon the people and tear into them. Death goes all around and holds a great harvest; it mows over millions.

And now comes the great breaking asunder of Christendom. Their kingdoms will disintegrate and be torn up. Terrible confusion and fear comes over the followers of Christ. They must recognize that all of these attacks are basically attacks against Christ and his Word. Yes, that this Word obviously has no power over them. The previous war has confused thousands, even millions, about Christ, even among those who took his Word seriously, and now see themselves so bitterly disappointed. Read war letters; read the compilation of reports from the working class about church and Christendom that was published by a Berlin pastor. All these things are written there so that anyone can read them. "The war has shown me that Christ is not right." "The war robbed me of faith in God." "Since the war, I know that belief is madness." Those are clear words about war and the church of Christ—it is very pharisaical to simply say here: "Well now, they never really had a right faith." Dear congregation, indeed, one must have had a right faith to feel so clearly that one's faith is destroyed. And who among us wishes to say that he or she has the right faith which nothing, absolutely nothing, can jeopardize. If someone thinks that he or she has such a faith may he or she ponder over it very sharply, as to whether this faith has become more one of indifference which nothing can disturb. Therefore, let there be caution with such pharisaic reproaches. Didn't those millions also have a right to Christ, who was snatched away from them? What are we going to say about this, we who were pulled into this event of 1914–1918, and thus are partially to blame for the fact their faith was taken from them?

God's way in the world leads to the cross and through the cross to life. Therefore, do not be afraid; fear not; be faithful! But what is meant here by being faithful is, namely, to enter this furious storm even to exhaustion, even to vexation, even to the call to martyrdom for the Word of Christ, so that there will be peace, so that there will be love, so that there will be salvation, and so that he is our peace and that God is a God of peace. And the more they storm, the more shall we call. And the more we call, the more wildly will they storm because, where the Word of Christ is truly said, there the world feels that it is either a destructive madness or rather a destructive truth, which is a matter then of life and death. Where truly peace has been spoken, there the war must doubly rage, since it perceives that it is to be finished off. Christ wishes to be its death.

But the more passionately and the more faithfully must the church of Christ stand with its Lord and preach his Word of peace, even if it goes through abuse and persecution. It knows that its Lord had to go to the cross. But now it understands the promise that Jesus is for it. The war will not be the end. But the war must exist, so that the end comes. "The gospel of the Kingdom will be preached in the whole world as a witness to all people, and then the end will come." Here our vision broadens, and will be lifted up to the Lord who rules all, whom even the demons and devils must serve. War, sickness, and hunger must come so that the gospel of the kingdom of peace, of love and salvation may be said and heard so much more clearly and deeply. The evil powers must serve the gospel; the powers of enmity and of the nations' opposition must also serve, to bring the gospel to all nations, so that it may be heard by all; all these must serve the Kingdom which shall belong to all humankind. War serves peace, hatred serves love, the devil serves God, the cross serves life. And then, when that becomes manifest, then the end will come; then the Lord of the church will lay his hand of blessing and protection on them, as on his faithful servant.

The Day of National Mourning in the church! What does it mean? It means the raising up of the

> one great hope, from which we all live, the sermon concerning the Kingdom of God. It means that we see the past, about which we think today, with all its terrors and in all its godlessness and we are still not to be afraid, but we hear the sermon on peace. It means that all this must come about, so that the end comes, so that God remains the Lord. It means that we rightly mourn over the dead of the world war. When we stand in the same faithfulness in which they stood out there, so we now deliver the message of peace and preach so much louder, the kingdom on which account death had to come about. It means to look beyond the borders of our people, over the whole earth, and pray that the gospel of the Kingdom that sets an end to all war, will come to all peoples, and that then the end comes and Christ draws near.[17]

3. "The Church and the Peoples of the World": Address at the Meeting of the Ecumenical Council of Christian Churches given during the Ecumenical Conference at Fanø, Denmark, August 28, 1934[18]

Background Context

Bonhoeffer's development into an outspoken advocate for peace reached a high point in his presentation at the ecu-

17. TF, 201–4.

18. The text of this address is drawn from Bonhoeffer's collected writings from that period published as *London: 1933–1935* (DBWE 13), 307–10 (hereafter *L*). Keith Clements, editor, also includes in this section of *L*, the valuable thesis paper that Bonhoeffer composed in preparation for the address he was to deliver at the Fanø conference.

menical conference in Fanø, entitled "The Church and the People of the World." Even in the contemporary world, few sermons, conferences, or public statements can match the fervor and intensity of Bonhoeffer's words at that conference in September 1934. Bonhoeffer was speaking to a formidable congregation of Christian leaders and ecumenical delegates drawn from several nations representing an extremely diverse variety of Christian denominations. For Bonhoeffer, the typical focus of these ecumenical gatherings was on the reconciliation of dogmatic, liturgical differences, which, though admirable in itself, was not in his opinion the most pressing need of the day. He had already perceived that, under Hitler, the German nation seemed to be heading for another round of violence in its quest to recapture the military glory lost in the Great War. Bonhoeffer's approach in 1934 to the issue of how these ecumenical delegates could help bring about peace was, first of all, to admit to his distinguished audience that, though the ecumenical church's primary mission did not deal with politics as such, nonetheless, its decisions had a significant impact on the world that politicians as well as churches were supposed to serve.

But even given this reservation, Bonhoeffer reminded his colleagues that the churches had received an unmistakable mandate from God at the advent of Jesus Christ that there shall be peace on earth. Unfortunately, the history of Christendom was severely burdened by the unquestioning

---

Another version of this address has been included in the "sermons" section of *TF*, 227–29. The TF version changes Bonhoeffer's original by using gender inclusive language in pronominal references to God. The DBWE volume offers helpful critical notes as well as the most accurate rendition of Bonhoeffer's original address, hence quotations in this section follow the DBWE 13 text rather than the TF version.

acceptance of warfare. The common citizens' blindness to the horrors of warfare was abetted by the wily parsing of God's command to the effect that Christians had been made to believe God couldn't really have meant what was said so directly in the scriptures about God's will for peace on earth. Surely God didn't actually intend peace without war and the attainment of military glory? Didn't God also commission leaders to provide security, even if that meant tanks and poison gas? Or that most serious question that Bonhoeffer held up as their most devilish rhetorical deception: "Did God say you should not protect your own people? Did God say you should leave your own a prey to the enemy?" To which Bonhoeffer replied clearly and forcefully that "God did not say all that. What God has said is that there shall be peace among men—that we shall obey Him without further question, that is what He means. He who questions the commandment of God before obeying has already denied Him."[19]

Bonhoeffer went on to say that there must be peace, because that is God's will for the mission of Christians and their churches. "This church of Christ in its ecumenical dimensions lives at one and the same time in all peoples, yet beyond all boundaries, whether national, political, social, or racial."[20] The word of Christ thus transcends all the separations that are often invoked to legitimate enmities and justify wars based on distinctions of blood, class, or language in addition to the usual pretexts invoked to "justify" attacking another nation, another people. Yet Christ identifies with all peoples to the effect that, as Bonhoeffer points out, Christians

19. L, 307–8.

20. L, 308.

who wage war are, in effect, using their weapons against Jesus Christ himself.[21]

Bonhoeffer then went over the practical strategies that nations, still reeling from the Great War, had brought into play to justify their own self-serving ways of keeping the peace: political treaties, money and investments, building up strong armies and arsenals. The scene was 1934, yet one might say that the same rationalizations exist in today's world. None of these can succeed, he said, because they confuse peace with security while the belligerent nations never deal with the one attitude necessary for peace, mutual trust. In an earlier ecumenical talk in Gland, Switzerland, he had denounced the political stratagem and insidious rationale of turning national security into an idol to be worshipped at all costs.[22]

In 1934, given the nations' historical penchant for settling their grievances against each other by militarized violence, Bonhoeffer urged the delegates of the World Alliance to be courageous, even daring, in their efforts at peace making. "For peace," he said, "must be dared. It is the great venture."[23] Who would summon the nations to peace? Neither individual Christians whose witness was too easily dismissed by the powers of the militarized world, nor the few individual churches whose peace activism and resistance to war was isolated and ineffective against the forces of internecine hatred and governmental sanctions. He concluded with a challenge to the ecumenical delegates that their prominence in the world as representing the church of Jesus Christ demanded that they undertake the mission of peacemaking. He asked

21. L, 308.

22. TF, 202.

23. L, 309.

them to live up to their claim to be the Ecumenical Council of the Church of Jesus Christ. They had the best opportunity and the responsibility to speak out courageously and convincingly so that the nations would be forced to hear. It was in the church's power, he declared, to take the "weapons from their sons," to forbid war, and to proclaim "the peace of Christ against the raging world."[24] This was a gauntlet thrown at the churches to undertake the mission of condemning war for its denial of Jesus Christ and his teachings. For Bonhoeffer, this was the most urgent task of the ecumenical conference and a task given them by God that overshadowed all their attempts to work out their dogmatic and liturgical differences.

One of Bonhoeffer's students, present at the conference, remarked that Bonhoeffer had leapt so far ahead of everyone else in the cause of peace that none were able to follow him. But he left them with an uneasy conscience.[25] After the Second World War with its death toll of over fifty million people, mostly civilians, Bonhoeffer's words would be taken seriously and incorporated into the official policies of the World Council of Churches, the successor of the ecumenical body to which Bonhnoeffer belonged as "Youth Secretary" and representative of the young ministers of Germany.

Text of the Conference

> "I will hear what God the Lord will speak: for he will speak peace unto his people, and to his saints" (Ps 85:8)

24. L, 309.
25. Cited in CML, 210.

Between the twin crags of nationalism and internationalism ecumenical Christendom calls upon her Lord and asks his guidance. Nationalism and internationalism have to do with political necessities and possibilities. The ecumenical church, however, does not concern itself with these things, but with the commandments of God, and regardless of consequences it transmits these commandments to the world.

Our task as theologians, accordingly consists only in accepting this commandment as a binding one, not as a question open to discussion. Peace on earth is not a problem, but a commandment given at Christ's coming. There are two ways of reacting to this command from God: the unconditional, blind obedience of action, or the hypocritical question of the Serpent: "Yea, hath God said . . . ? This question is the mortal enemy of obedience, and therefore the mortal enemy of all real peace. "Hath God not said . . . ? Has God not understood human nature well enough to know that wars must occur in this world, like laws of nature? Must God not have meant that we should talk about peace, to be sure, but that it is not to be literally translated into action? Must God not really have said that we should work for peace, of course, but also make ready tanks and poison gas for security?" And then perhaps the most serious question: "Did God say you should not protect your own people? Did God say you should leave your own a prey to the enemy?"

No, God did not say all that. What He has said is that there shall be peace among men—that we shall obey Him without further question, that is what He means. He who questions the commandment of God before obeying has already denied Him.

There shall be peace because of the Church of Christ, for the sake of which the world exists. And this Church of Christ lives at one and the same time in all peoples, yet beyond all boundaries, whether national, political, social, or racial. And the brothers who make up this Church are bound together, through the commandment of the one Lord Christ, whose Word they hear, more inseparably than men are bound by all the ties of common history, of blood, of class and of language. All these ties, which are part of our world, are valid ties, not indifferent; but in the presence of Christ, they are not ultimate bonds. For the members of the ecumenical Church, in so far as they hold to Christ, His word, His commandment of peace is more holy, more inviolable than the most revered words and works of the natural world. For they know that whoso is not able to hate father and mother for His sake is not worthy of Him, and lies if he calls himself after Christ's name. These brothers in Christ obey His word; they do not doubt or question, but keep His commandment of peace. "They are not ashamed, in defiance of the world, even to speak of eternal peace. They cannot take up arms against Christ himself—yet this is what they do if they take up arms against one another! Even in anguish and distress of conscience there is for them no escape from the commandment of Christ that there shall be peace.

How does peace come about? Through a system of political treaties? Through the investment of international capital in different countries? Through the big banks, through money? Or through universal peaceful rearmament in order to guarantee peace? Through none of these, for the single reason that in all of them peace is confused with safety. There is no way to peace along the way of safety. For peace must be dared. It is the great venture. It can never be made safe. Peace is the opposite of security. To demand guarantees is to mistrust, and this mistrust in turn brings forth war. To look for guarantees is to want to protect oneself. Peace means to give oneself to the law of God, wanting no security, but in faith and obedience laying the destiny of the nations in the hand of Almighty God, not trying to direct it for selfish purposes. Battles are won, not with weapons, but with God. They are won where the way leads to the cross. Which of us can say he knows what it might mean for the world if one nation should meet the aggressor, not with weapons in hand, but praying, defenseless, and for that very reason protected by "a bulwark never failing"?

Once again, how will peace come? Who will call us to peace so that the world will hear, will have to hear? so that all peoples may rejoice? The individual Christian cannot do it. When all around are silent, he can indeed raise his voice and bear witness, but the powers of this world stride over him without a word. The individual church, too, can witness and suffer—oh, if it only would!—but is also is suffocated by the power of hate. Only the one great Ecumenical Council of the Holy Church of Christ over all the world can speak out so that the world, though it gnash its teeth, will have to hear, so that the peoples will rejoice because the Church of Christ in the name of Christ has taken the weapons from the hands of their sons, forbidden war, and proclaimed the peace of Christ against the raging world.

Why do we fear the fury of the world powers? Why don't we take the power from them and give it back to Christ? We can still do it today. The Ecumenical Council is in session; it can send out to all believers this radical call to peace. The nations are waiting for it in the East and in the West. Must we be put to shame by non-Christian peoples in the East?[26] Shall we desert the individuals who are risking their lives for this message? The hour is late. The world is choked with weapons, and dreadful is the distrust which looks out of all men's eyes. The trumpets of war may blow tomorrow. For what are we waiting? Do we want to become involved in this guilt as never before? . . .

We want to give the world a whole word, not a half word—a courageous word, a Christian word. We want to pray that this word may be given us, today. Who knows if we shall see each other again another year?[27]

26. A reference to the peace activism and teachings of Mohandas Gandhi, whose nonviolent, pacifist resistance tactics had succeeded in mobilizing the citizens of India against the imperialistic domination of Great Britain.

27. L, 307–10.

Questions

1. Do you agree with Bonhoeffer's assertion that the church renounces obedience to Jesus Christ should it sanction war?

2. Are his words still true today that the arms race and the development of weaponry to guarantee peace and security is demonic? He also asserts that national security has become an idol. Given the military budget and the neglect of social programs today, do you agree?

3. What does Bonhoeffer mean by his complaint that the powers for war use the name "Christ" against the true Christ? Why does he claim that war is a rebellion against Jesus Christ? Is Bonhoeffer correct in calling for repentance for having engaged in a war against other nations?

4. Is Bonhoeffer correct in blaming the churches for the violence in the Great War by having declared it "just"? What criteria for a war to be declared "just" may have been violated in the wars of the twentieth century and in the present war in Iraq?

5. In your opinion how effective would a massive church protest against war be without the exertion of some coercive force along the lines suggested by Bonhoeffer?

6. If one believes in the mystical body of Jesus Christ, as Bonhoeffer does, would his argument have validity, that the killing that goes on in war is in reality the killing anew of Jesus Christ?

7. What does Bonhoeffer mean by his declaration that "peace must be dared; it is the great venture"? What is the personal cost of undertaking such a venture?

Bibliography*

In this bibliography are listed the collection of primary sources that make up the 17 volumes of Bonhoeffer's collected writings in their general reference under the titles Dietrich Bonhoeffer Werke (DBW) for the German editions and Dietrich Bonhoeffer Works English Edition (DBWE). Below the list of the DBWE are the volumes used or referred to in this book. Although the title of this book is *Reading Bonhoeffer*, it is indispensable for the most complete and accurate reading/interpretation of Dietrich Bonhoeffer, from his earliest years to his death, to read the collected writings listed here. These editions offer fully accurate translations and provide the critical apparatus necessary to fully understand the historical context and Bonhoeffer's original intent in his entire literary legacy.

Dietrich Bonhoeffer Werke (DBW). Edited by Eberhard Bethge et al. 17 vols. Munich: Chr. Kaiser Verlag, 1986–1999.

Dietrich Bonhoeffer Works English Edition (DBWE). Edited by Wayne Whitson Floyd Jr., Victoria J. Barnett, et al. 16 vols. Minneapolis: Fortress, 1995–.

* The author acknowledges the assistance of Dr. Clifford J. Green, Executive Director of the DBWE, for his invaluable advice and assistance in constructing this bibliographical section.

DBWE

SC (DBWE 1)	*Sanctorum Communio*
AB (DBWE 2)	*Act and Being*
CF (DBWE 3)	*Creation and Fall*
D (DBWE 4)	*Discipleship*
LT (DBWE 5)	*Life Together*
PB (DBWE 5)	*Prayerbook of the Bible*
E (DBWE 6)	*Ethics*
FT (DBWE 7)	*Fiction from Tegel Prison*
YB (DBWE 9)	*The Young Bonhoeffer: 1918–1927*
BN (DBWE 10)	*Barcelona, Berlin, New York: 1928–1931*
L (DBWE 13)	*London: 1933–1935*
CI (DBWE 16)	*Conspiracy and Imprisonment: 1940–1945*

In Process

LPP (DBWE 8)	*Letters and Papers from Prison*
(DBWE 11)	*Ecumenical, Academic and Pastoral Work: 1931–1932*
(DBWE 12)	*Berlin: 1933*
(DBWE 14)	*Theological Education at Finkenwalde: 1935–1937*
(DBWE 15)	*Theological Education Underground: 1937–1940*

Primary Sources Cited

Illegale Theologenausbildung: Finkenwalde 1935–1937. DBW 14. Edited by Otto Dudzus and Jürgen Henkys with Sabine Bobert-Stützel, Dirk Schultz, and Ilse Tödt. Munich: Kaiser, 1996. (See DBWE 14 above.)

Sanctorum Communio: A Theological Study of the Sociology of the Church. DBWE 1. Edited by Clifford J. Green. Translated by Reinhard Krauss and Nancy Lukens. Minneapolis: Fortress, 1998.

Act and Being: Transcendental Philosophy and Ontology in Systematic Theology. DBWE 2. Edited by Wayne Whitson Floyd, Jr. Translated by H. Martin Rumscheidt. Minneapolis: Fortress, 1996.

Christ the Center (CC). A New Translation by Edwin H. Robertson. San Francisco: HarperSanFrancisco, 1978.

London: 1933–1935. DBWE 13. Edited by Keith Clements. Translated by Isabel Best and Douglas W. Stott. Minneapolis: Fortress, 2007.

Discipleship. DBWE 4. Edited by Geffrey B. Kelly and John D. Godsey. Translated by Barbara Green and Reinhard Krauss. Minneapolis: Fortress, 2001.

Life Together and Prayerbook of the Bible. DBWE 5. Edited by Geffrey B. Kelly. Translated by Daniel W. Bloesch. Minneapolis: Fortress, 1996.

Ethics. DBWE 6. Edited by Clifford J. Green. Translated by Reinhard Krauss, Charles C. West and Douglas W. Stott. Minneapolis: Fortress, 2005.

Letters and Papers from Prison (LPP). Edited by Eberhard Bethge. Translated by Reginald Fuller, Frank Clarke, et al. New York: Macmillan, 1971.

A Testament to Freedom: The Essential Writings of Dietrich Bonhoeffer (TF). Edited by Geffrey B. Kelly and F. Burton Nelson. Rev. ed. San Francisco: HarperSanFrancisco, 1995.

No Rusty Swords: Letters, Lectures, and Notes, 1928–1936. Collected Works of Dietrich Bonhoeffer 1. Edited and translated by Edwin H. Robertson. London: Collins, 1965.

Secondary Sources Cited in This Book

Bethge, Eberhard. *Dietrich Bonhoeffer: A Biography* (DB). Revised and edited by Victoria J. Barnett. Minneapolis: Fortress, 2000.

Kelly, Geffrey B. and F. Burton Nelson. *The Cost of Moral Leadership: The Spirituality of Dietrich Bonhoeffer* (CML). Grand Rapids: Eerdmans, 2002.

Kelly, Geffrey B. *Liberating Faith: Bonhoeffer's Message for Today* (LF). 1984. Reprinted, Eugene, OR: Wipf & Stock, 2002.

Other Secondary Sources Cited

Augustine. *Confessions*. Translated by Maria Boulding, OSB. Vintage Spiritual Classics. New York: Random House, 1998.

Best, Sigismund Payne. *The Venlo Incident.* New York: Hutchinson, 1950; the section on Bonhoeffer is now also found in *Dietrich Bonhoeffer Yearbook* 3. Munich: Gütersloher, 2008, 109–39.

Bethge, Eberhard. "Dietrich Bonhoeffer and the Jews." In *Ethical Responsibility: Bonhoeffer's Legacy to the Churches*, edited by John D. Godsey and Geffrey B. Kelly, 43–96. New York: Mellen, 1981.

Dupré, Louis. *Kierkegaard As Theologian.* New York: Sheed and Ward, 1963.

Green, Clifford J. *Bonhoeffer: A Theology of Sociality.* Grand Rapids: Eerdmans, 1999.

———. "Pacifism and Tyrannicide: Bonhoeffer's Christian Peace Ethic." *Studies in Christian Ethics* 18 (2005) 31–47.

Kelly, Geffrey B. "Who Stands Firm?" *Weavings: A Journal of the Christian Spiritual Life* 15 (2000) 33–39.

Nelson, F. Burton. "The Relationship of Jean Lasserre to Dietrich Bonhoeffer's Peace Concerns in the Struggle of Church and Culture." *Union Seminary Quarterly Review* 40:1–2 (1985) 71–84.

Shaw, George Bernard. "Common Sense about the War." In *Shaw on Religion: Irreverent Observations by a Man of Great Faith*, edited by Warren S. Smith, 60–61. New York: Dodd, Mead & Co., 1967.

Sorum, Jonathan D. "Cheap Grace, Costly Grace, and Just Plain Grace." *Lutheran Forum* 27 (1993) 20.

Bibliographies

There are available several up-to-date and helpful bibliographies of secondary source material. An electronic bibliography of primary sources by Bonhoeffer and the secondary literature on Bonhoeffer is available through the Burke Library, Union Theological Seminary, New York City. This is the most comprehensive and up-to-date bibliography for English language sources. It is updated annually from the "Bibliography Update" published in the winter issue of the *Newsletter of the International Bonhoeffer Society, English Language Section* (see Dean Skelley, editor, P.O. Box 160879, San Antonio, TX

78280-2395). To access the bibliography, search "Bonhoeffer Bibliography" in Google for the URL of the online bibliography. In addition, each issue of the *Dietrich Bonhoeffer Yearbook*, which is published every couple of years, also contains a continuation and update of the *International Bonhoeffer Bibliography*, edited by Ernst Feil and Barbara Fink, and published by Chr. Kaiser/ Gütersloher Verlagshaus, Munich, in 1998. What is more, the *Yearbook* publishes new documents by and related to Bonhoeffer that have been discovered since the completion of the Dietrich Bonhoeffer Werke, as well as articles containing Bonhoeffer research and interpretation.

See also the sources listed in Clifford Green's *Bonhhoeffer: A Theology of Sociality* and in *A Testament to Freedom*, edited by Kelly and Nelson, listed above. A dated, but quite remarkable, bibliography was published by Clifford J. Green in 1976. See his "Bonhoeffer Bibliography: English Language Sources," *Union Seminary Quarterly Review* 31 (1976) 227–60. Although it is not a bibliography per se, Stephen R. Haynes's wide-ranging commentary and critique of the secondary literature under the various categories he detects in the way writers have interpreted Bonhoeffer is helpful in recognizing the amazing diversity of interpretations extant and growing. His book is entitled *The Bonhoeffer Phenomenon: Portraits of a Protestant Saint*, published by Fortress Press in 2004.